CODENAME
D.O.U.C.H.E.B.A.G.

A NOVEL BY
FRANK CONNIFF

Published By
Podhouse 90 Press
ISBN: 978-0-692-16292-7

Design, Typesetting and Cover Design by Len Peralta

PART ONE

The Special Senate Committee To Investigate Domestic Terrorism has recently obtained a document pertaining to the recent incident in Aspen, Colorado. It is the Twitter feed of General John Stone of the United States Army, Ret. We submit it here as evidence in our ongoing investigation.

@GeneralStone As a General in the armed forces of these United States, I have shown a great devotion to my country, serving on the battlefront in many wars.

 @GeneralStone Granted, they've mainly been hashtag wars, but any kind of war is hell, and I have the carpal tunnel syndrome to prove it.

 @GeneralStone But I'm not just a warrior on social media, I'm an actual Army General who has also served in the front lines of Cable News programming and Sunday Morning talk shows.

 @GeneralStone And let's not forget my service in Operation Desert Storm. I say this not out of any egotistical self-aggrandizement, but because of a simple historical truth: most people have forgotten my service in Operation Desert Storm.

 @GeneralStone But I was essential. There would be no Operation Desert Storm without me, because I'm the General who came up with the name.

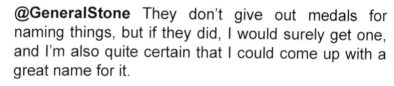 **@GeneralStone** They don't give out medals for naming things, but if they did, I would surely get one, and I'm also quite certain that I could come up with a great name for it.

 @GeneralStone How about The Congressional Medal of Branding? See, I'm quite good at this sort of thing.

 @GeneralStone My Desert Storm brainstorm happened in the early 90s when I was in the Pentagon Situation Room.

 @General Stone The "Situation Room" is the nickname I came up with for the canteen where all the vending machines were. Stormin' Norman Schwarzkopf was banging his fist against the glass because the Nutrageous Bar he sought was not obeying orders and falling in line with his coin-operated command.

@GeneralStone Oh, you'd better believe that candy bar eventually did as it was told. When General Schwarzkopf says, "fall down into the vending slot, Mister!" the chocolatey treat says, "how low?" I'll bet he made that sweet confection drop and give him twenty before he even ate the damn thing.

 @GeneralStone Anyway, I told the General that we should name the mission in the desert something like Operation Kill Kill Win Win, and he took that idea, slightly tweaked it, and thus, Operation Desert Storm.,

 @GeneralStone So he definitely followed my suggestion to use the word, "Operation," and I've always been proud of that.

 @GeneralStone This is the sort of strategic Patton-like thinking that made me a favored military expert on countless cable news shows.

 @GeneralStone Plus, my crew-cutted chiseled pale white face conveyed the perfect telegenic military look. And since I was a Talking Head, the camera never saw that my body wasn't exactly in Seal Team Six condition.

 @GeneralStone I was coveted by the producers of these programs for the carefully considered opinions I was able to come up with off the top of my head.

 @GeneralStone You may have heard the expression, Old soldiers never die, they just become TV Pundits or consultants for weapons manufacturers. I was the living embodiment of this truth.

 @GeneralStone This phase of my life began back in 2000 when the Supreme Court decided that George W. Bush had won the election, thus paving the way for Dick Cheney to become President.

@GeneralStone That was right around the time I retired from the service and published my super-patriotic book, America: Why She Makes Me Cum.

 @GeneralStone It was a blockbuster bestseller, and only partially because my publisher, Regnery Books, purchased thousands of copies in bulk.

 @GeneralStone And then came an even bigger break for me - The Iraq War. Our Commander in Chief, Dick Cheney, had my back. The name Dick might be a euphemism for penis, but for me, the name Cheney is a euphemism for patriotism.

 @GeneralStone And I didn't have to just depend on my salary from TV news shows, there were other corporations besides the broadcast journalism industry also eager to cash in on the war, and more than willing to solicit my services based on my high media profile.

 @GeneralStone I was known as someone who spent a lot of time hanging around Pentagon vending machines, so confectionary companies began to contact me about getting their products into the burgeoning Middle East Quagmire market.

 @GeneralStone I was hired to work as a consultant for Atrocities Novelties, a company whose specialty is moving into war zones and opening Joke Shops that sell toys, prank gifts and candy.

 @GeneralStone I was the team leader on a military contract they received that involved the development of cocktail napkins with racy jokes that were distributed to Iraqi war orphans.

 @GeneralStone There was no possible way these kids would understand the jokes, and they had no use for cocktail napkins either. There was absolutely no practical aspect to this initiative, which is why the

Pentagon authorized a shit-ton of money to manufacture the product.

 @GeneralStone Was I a war profiteer? I never had time to figure that out, because I was too busy making money hand over fist from all the death and carnage in Iraq.

 @GeneralStone And remember, you can't say war profiteer without profit.

 @GeneralStone Capitalism is all about profit, and profits are as American as Pinkberry. (I would say American as apple pie, but I spearheaded an initiative to open a frozen yogurt stand at Guantanamo, so I want to stay on-brand.)

 @GeneralStone There is a theory among certain Americans that it is somehow unethical for a war profiteer to go on cable news shows and promote a war that he is profiteering from.

 @GeneralStone Fortunately for me, I've never met a TV executive at any cable or broadcast news network who gave a good goddamn that I was profiting from the war. My conflict of interest was of no interest to anyone.

 @GeneralStone Most of the on-air predictions I made and advice I gave about military strategy turned out to be 100% wrong. I only mention this as an explanation for why I was asked to come on those cable news shows again and again for so many years.

 @GeneralStone Like a lot of other Army brass, I spent much of the war in what had become one of the prime military outposts of the modern era — the TV studio green room.

@GeneralStone There's no denying I had it really good for a while there. As long as the only consequence of my punditry was the deaths of thousands of innocent people, my job was secure and there would always be a place for me in Cable and Network News.

 @GeneralStone But then, out of the blue, it all fell apart, and what brought me down was the last thing you'd expect to be a problem in the world of TV news: a lie.

 @GeneralStone I assume you've all heard the story of Brian Williams and how he fibbed about being under enemy fire in a war zone on a helicopter, right?

 @GeneralStone He wasn't there and neither was I, but even though it never happened, it's the one combat skirmish that I've ever been a casualty of.

 @GeneralStone It started one night when I was a guest on his NBC Nightly News show and he happened to make eye contact with me just as he was telling his helicopter story, so he decided to include me in his heroic saga.

 @GeneralStone Why not? When you're making shit up as you go along, anyone and anything can be a part of your story.

 @GeneralStone I didn't think there'd be any harm in me riding to glory with Brian on his fictional whirlybird, so I fired up The Ride Of The Valkyries in my head and hopped on board.

 @GeneralStone At the time, it seemed advantages to me. I calculated it could bring more attention to my company, which was promoting a new brand of gum. We tried to get the rights to the Bazooka Joe trademark but instead we ended up calling it Grenade Launcher Larry.

@GeneralStone I came up with a great slogan for Veterans who had come home from the war, "It's PTSDelicious!"

 @GeneralStone As you may already know, Brian Williams was the number one TV anchor at the time. I figured associating myself with him would be good for me and good for the brands I was promoting.

 @GeneralStone What could possibly go wrong?

 @GeneralStone Well, as it turned out, the actual veterans who were on the actual chopper that Brian Williams claimed he was on, and that I said I was on, too, pointed out a slight discrepancy in Brian's story — it was complete bullshit.

 @GeneralStone Well, the resultant outrage was devastating for Brian. He lost everything, except his job, his home, his million dollar salary, and his luxurious lifestyle. But he lost everything else.

 @GeneralStone NBC sent a message that all its broadcast and cable anchors were put on notice: if you treat the sacred profession of journalism with a complete disregard for the truth, you will be slightly inconvenienced and forced to work later hours.

 @GeneralStone I, on the other hand, was shit-canned. There were plenty of other military experts on cable TV who unethically profited from the war and talked out of their asses, so there was nothing unique about me. I was expendable.

 @GeneralStone And just like that, I was washed up as a pundit. It was a huge loss for me, like watching your best buddy die on the battlefield, except in my case the battlefield was a TV studio and my best buddy was a huge pile of money.

@GeneralStone The first casualty of war is the truth, and now I wasn't allowed to lie about that anymore.

 @GeneralStone I mean, what's the point of even having an opinion if you can't give it in front of a TV camera? I don't see the point.

 @GeneralStone Now I was forced to interact with the so-called real world. But I was an experienced cable TV news pundit, so the idea of engaging in honest human discourse with other living beings seemed degrading to me.

 @GeneralStone What was I to do?

 @GeneralStone I was left with limited career options.

 @GeneralStone I wasn't welcomed on TV anymore, so what was in store for me? A podcast? No thank you! For a military man, that's the equivalent of being a in a Vietnamese Prisoner of War camp, but with less ability to monetize the experience.

 @GeneralStone I could write and reflect and become part of a respected Washington, D.C. think tank. Once again, no thank you. That's just a Vietnamese Prisoner of War camp with a bow tie.

 @GeneralStone I know I'm sounding bitter, and it's true, I was becoming a negative person. Being away from TV punditry and not being able to Monday morning quarterback an overseas conflict on a daily basis was taking all the joy out of war.

 @GeneralStone In fact, war didn't seem real to me unless I could pontificate about it on national television. After all, if a tree falls in a forest, and there's no pundit to provide commentary, does it make a sound bite?

@GeneralStone Of course Atrocities Novelties dumped me the minute I lost my TV perch. I'm telling you, when you're a war profiteer and the profits stop rolling in, the futility of war suddenly seems pointless.

 @GeneralStone Cable and Network news is a world of wealth and luxury. The weapons manufacturers who employ TV anchors want their spokespeople to be well compensated. When you're expressing narratives that throw the lives of people halfway around the world into poverty, you can't look shabby.

 @GeneralStone Mainstream media mainly consists of millionaires hired by billionaires to report on what's going on with everyday Americans. And the last thing I wanted was to go back to being an everyday American.

 @GeneralStone I had to somehow find my way back in. A TV studio was a hill I had to once again take.

 @GeneralStone What a military man like me needed was a military operation.

 @GeneralStone I had seen a lot of combat. Granted, I had only seen it on overhead monitors in TV studios, but the point is, I had seen it.

 @GeneralStone I needed to go on a genuine, bonafide military operation. But what kind?

 @GeneralStone In the tradition of America's involvement in the Iraq War, it would have to be an objective that was easily winnable, or at least easy to describe as winnable long after it becomes clear to everyone that failure was not only an option but an inevitability.

@GeneralStone I knew I had to venture out of my comfort zone and find out what was happening in the real world. So I hit the Internet.

 @GeneralStone But not in my usual way, which often starts with the best intentions but ends with me clicking the "clear history" button.

 @GeneralStone I wasn't dealing in abstractions anymore. I was entering the reality-based community, which I had long disdained. But you can't destroy something if it doesn't exist in the first place.

 @GeneralStone And I found something to destroy. And I believe that destroying it will give me the rebirth I need.

 @GeneralStone The Grey Poupon Institute is an elitist think tank located in a chateau in the mountains of Aspen, Colorado at the exact center point between Malibu and the Hamptons. It doesn't get much more liberal and anti-American than that.

 @GeneralStone During my consultancy with Atrocities Novelties, I had some experience in the world of seasoning. We developed a product called Russian Collusion Dressing but we were a little bit ahead of the curve on that one.

 @GeneralStone I've always made a point of avoiding liberal-leaning condiments, and Grey Poupon mustard has been bringing socialism to sandwiches for way too long.

 @GeneralStone So it occurred to me that a tightly coordinated commando raid on the Grey Poupon Institute would be the ultimate act of patriotism.

 @GeneralStone And the exact right time to strike is upon us.

@GeneralStone The Aspen chateau contains the laboratory where grey poupon mustard is researched and developed. Every year the new mustard upgrade is presented to an exclusive group of liberal celebrities and progressive leaders. That date is coming up.

 @GeneralStone So I have found the perfect target for my commando mission. But you can't have a commando mission without commandoes.

 @GeneralStone Right now my next step is to find a rag tag group of Soldiers of Fortune ready for a top secret commando mission.

 @GeneralStone But all the rag tag groups of commandos for hire that I know are busy fighting public wars, secret wars, and moral equivalents of wars. So instead I searched for recruits from the world I knew.

 @GeneralStone The world of washed-up cable news pundits.

The twitter feed of cable television personality Bob McGlory is also pertinent to our ongoing investigation, so we present this document into the record of the Senate Committee.

 @BobMcGlory I'm not going to try and justify myself. I know what I did and what I didn't do. I didn't sexually harass any of those dozens women who had never met each other and who came forward with the exact same stories about me.

 @BobMcGlory I have done so much for women. No anchor in the cable news business has made more promises to more hot women about helping their careers than I have.

@BobMcGlory Being Bob McGlory, the most admired news anchor in cable, and host of the number one top rated show, The McGlory Hole, made me a target.

 @BobMcGlory I could go on and on about these harassing harpies, but the thing I hate most about predatory women is that they all tend to ignore me.

 @BobMcGlory As anybody knows who's seen the opening commentaries on my show, I am a very spiritual person, and not just because I cheated on my wife religiously.

 @BobMcGlory But the thing is, when you're as incredible a lover as I am, it would be downright cruel to deny women my essence. And people who've watched my broadcast know that I am all about the facts. So when I tell you I am amazing in bed, it is based on through investigative reporting.

 @BobMcGlory I interviewed many of the women I've made love to and they can all attest to the multiple orgasms that ricocheted within Marriott Rewards Suites throughout these United States of America. I'm just glad the women sleeping with me didn't also orgasm; that would have been overkill.

 @BobMcGlory You may have seen the news item where my ex-wife claimed I was not able to perform in bed. For this, I don't blame myself, I blame George Soros, and if you don't understand why, you just don't understand how the Deep State works.

 @BobMcGlory And don't believe for one minute that my ex-wife is some kind of feminist. I tried many times to get her to allow another chick to join us in the sack and she wasn't having it.

@BobMcGlory Despite all her lip service to the woman's movement, she gave absolutely no lip service to the other woman I wanted her to french-kiss in bed. Hypocrite.

 @BobMcGlory By the way, my ex-wife, of course, is super hot. You wouldn't expect a celebrity of my standing to settle for anything less. She was such a trophy that in my marriage vows I thanked the members of the academy.

 @BobMcGlory But is it my fault that I got bored having sex with her after a few weeks of marriage? I know my religion says that man must stay faithful to his wife, and I respect the words of the Bible, even though it's print media.

 @BobMcGlory I humbly believe that if Jesus came back to Earth, he would yell my name out while having sex. So I have reverently followed His words and His teachings during the moments in life that matter the most — when it's convenient to Me.

 @BobMcGlory But then a storm blew into my life, and God forgot to tell me to build an ark, which I can't help but think is an unfortunate example of our Lord and Savior being kind of a dick.

 @BobMcGlory You see, I had a segment producer in my employ who was really something else. She stood out from most of the other gals who worked at our network, because, for one thing, she was brunette.

 @BobMcGlory If you were a woman, and you weren't blonde, security alarms would go off when you entered the lobby of our cable news channel.

 @BobMcGlory But some brunettes and redheads were hired as part of our diversity outreach.

@BobMcGlory And although this particular brunette's clothes were a little loose-fitting for my taste, my investigative reporter instincts told me there was zero body fat underneath those willowy dresses.

 @BobMcGlory She was pale from ambition and her face conveyed an earnest serious intelligence. But despite this, I was attracted to her.

 @BobMcGlory Not that she was perfect. There was something about her that smacked of self-esteem, but I was willing to overlook this flaw and give her a chance anyway.

 @BobMcGlory But she did work under me, so I realized things might get complicated if I actually had her under me. So I did the ethical thing - rather than have an actual affair, I decided to instead masturbate while having work-related conversations with her at the office and on the phone.

 @BobMcGlory Now, I'm an old fashioned traditional values kind of guy. That's why when I had phone sex, I always made a point of having it on a landline.

 @BobMcGlory So when I called up this tragically brunette segment producer to discuss my show's daily rundown, I did it from my private panic room that I keep in my Westchester estate. It's in the basement right next to my echo chamber.

 @BobMcGlory I made it a regular routine to call up this segment producer every morning before I came in to the studio, and late at night after I got home. I did most of the talking, because she was a novice in the news business, and I was a mentor to her, which is why I did all the jerking-off.

 @BobMcGlory Of course a lot of what I said to her might sound a bit odd when taken out of context.

@BobMcGlory The intense detail I went into about how I wanted her to rub middle eastern dipping sauces all over my body might not have been standard journalism school curriculum, but it gave her a chance to familiarize herself with international issues.

 @BobMcGlory The trouble I got into began when suddenly in the middle of a conversation it seemed like my landline went dead. Did my segment producer, someone who WORKED FOR ME, actually just hang up on me without giving me the courtesy of waiting till I ejaculated?

 @BobMcGlory Needless to say, I drove into Manhattan that day with every intention of taking a shower in my office bathroom, then walking around in an open robe while I berated her for her lack of professionalism.

 @BobMcGlory But then she ambushed me. She revealed that she had been recording our phone conversations, which really pissed me off, because this was before I became a podcaster, so at the time I hated the idea of giving anyone free content.

 @BobMcGlory Her lawyer was there at the office and he played the tapes back to me.

 @BobMcGlory As I listened to our conversations, I had to admit that my descriptions of her sandpapering my scrotum with industrial strength bristle brushes might be misconstrued as somewhat salacious in nature for people who have no understanding of nuance.

 @BobMcGlory She was pushing me up against a wall. Not literally, of course, but metaphorically, and isn't it just like an uptight feminist to do metaphorical shit.

@BobMcGlory I just wanted her and her lawyer out of my office. The accusations that I was some sort of pervert were deeply offensive to me. Plus, I had an urgent desire to be alone so I could listen to the tapes and jack-off all over again.

 @BobMcGlory But before I did anything else, I had to prove my innocence. So I paid her a lot of money and now that she was legally restricted from saying what had really happened, I was cleared of all wrongdoing.

 @BobMcGlory I did learn an important lesson. I learned that some women are so unprincipled they will record you while you are having unsolicited phone sex with them. The real tragedy is that this has completely turned me off to phone sex.

 @BobMcGlory Look, I'm just a regular Joe, a populist, a man of the people, so why should I have to go to Human Resources?

 @BobMcGlory And what happened when I did go? I show up for the session and the Human Resources chick is an absolute fucking knock out! She had bazongas the size of Texas and Florida, and those are both red states, so you know I was excited.

 @BobMcGlory I won't go into detail about what happened next, but suffice to say, PC culture has now gotten to the point where you can't even ask a Human Resources director to cup your balls without it becoming a whole thing.

 @BobMcGlory You've already read about what happened next. I had to leave my post as cable's number one newsman. It was a tragedy that this country will not soon recover from. It was like another 9/11, but this time with tragic consequences.

@BobMcGlory And my misfortune had an impact on the economy as well.

 @BobMcGlory All the agreements that women had signed restricting them from speaking publicly about their interactions with me were now moot, and this had a devastating effect on companies that manufacture non-disclosure agreements.

 @BobMcGlory Despite all this, things are good, really they are. I started a podcast and it is doing great. It has a loyal listenership and we're building up an audience with our premium subscriptions and we are thinking of starting a Kickstarter and

 @BobMcGlory Oh, who am I kidding? Podcasting is a living death! It's like a suicide note that's available on SoundCloud.

 @BobMcGlory I have got to do something that will make me relevant again! Something bold! Something big! Something that will make me worthy of one of those cheap looking alarm logos on the Drudge Report again!

 @BobMcGlory I just heard from General Stone. I used to have him on my show, and the idea he hit me up with about a commando mission is the most interesting offer I've heard all day, and not just because it's the only offer I've heard all day.

This Senate Investigative Committee must practice due diligence and examine all documents that are relevant to this case. So as much as we'd prefer not to, we must enter the Twitter feed of You Tube prankster Monty Washburn into evidence

 @MontyWashburn If you are a liberal elitist, you are no fan of mine. If, on the other hand, you are a salt-of-the-earth conservative, you haven't let your complete lack of exposure to my work diminish your deep appreciation of it.

@MontyWashburn I just happen to be at that point in my career where the people who admire me the most are the ones who've never heard of me.

 @MontyWashburn I'm not as famous as I'd like to be, because my unique brand of humor is not what is known in comedy lingo as "funny."

 @MontyWashburn But nobody is better at exposing the folly of liberal elitists than yours truly. And it's the nature of my particular set of skills that I am able to bring down the progressive elite without resorting to ideology or reason or common sense.

 @MontyWashburn I achieve my ends through tomfoolery and public pranking. I would say that I am the spoonful of sugar that helps the medicine go down, except I am opposed to healthcare, and therefore to medicine.

 @MontyWashburn I've done some awesome pranks in my day. Like the time I rang the doorbell at the front entrance of DNC headquarters and then ran away before they could answer.

 @MontyWashburn The video I made of it had over 50 views on You Tube, so it was cool to be part of something that went viral.

 @MontyWashburn But more importantly, that prank made a great point: the Democrat party is always saying that nothing can distract them from helping poor people and black people, and yet when they hear a doorbell ring, they drop everything they're doing to go see who's at the door.

 @MontyWashburn They are so dishonest.

@MontyWashburn Before I began my career of hijinks-based activism, I started out as a stand-up comedian. But I am here to tell you that conservatives are not welcome in the world of show business.

 @MontyWashburn If you are an entertainer who never entertains anyone, the comedy community holds that as a mark against you. That's how left-wing they are.

 @MontyWashburn I did some really edgy material that the high-hat liberal open mic elitists just did not care for.

 @MontyWashburn My "What's the deal with women?" bit, in which I had the temerity to ask, "What's the deal with women?" was met with silence just because it didn't have the kind of politically correct elements so precious to hipster poseurs, like a point or a punch line.

 @MontyWashburn You have to understand that sometimes what's funny on the page is not necessarily what's funny on the stage. But my talent was that I could take something not funny on the page, and then make it seem just as unfunny on the stage.

 @MontyWashburn Don't get me wrong, my bits are really funny, just not in a way that ever gets laughs.

 @MontyWashburn My material is tricky because I've found that people appreciate my comedy much better when they don't have a sense of humor.

 @MontyWashburn So comedy clubs were not my ideal forum. You Tube was a much better vehicle for my button down brand of breezy irreverence. As a comedian it was quite freeing to no longer be burdened with the pressure to provide comedy.

@MontyWashburn I pulled some good pranks. In addition to the aforementioned doorbell bit, I shot a video where I used food stamps at Arby's, proving once and for all that that they can be used to buy other things besides food.

 @MontyWashburn I also captured footage of Barack Obama high-fiving another black person, proving that he's blacker than he makes himself out to be. Some say that clip didn't make a difference, but I would point out that he hasn't run for President again, has he?

 @MontyWashburn Another fun prank was when I went to a government agency and applied for a disaster relief loan. But I hadn't been in any disaster and I didn't need any loan, so guess what happened?

 @MontyWashburn They turned me down.

 @MontyWashburn But here's the kicker: they GENTLY turned me down. In a respectful, sympathetic way. And I got it all on tape. Zing! Nailed them!

 @MontyWashburn After I released a video proving that all of the people appearing in the movie GeoStorm were in fact crisis actors, I assumed I had arrived. But unfortunately, when you assume, you make a person and possibly another person come off in a bad light.

 @MontyWashburn And it shouldn't surprise you to hear that the mainstream media had no interest in my videos. I was using satire to create comedy content that wasn't funny, and yet the entertainment industry big shots were not giving me credit for this innovation.

 @MontyWashburn Many people accused me of spreading misinformation. But remember, you can't spell "misinformation" without "information."

@MontyWashburn All of this work I was doing came from a pure altruistic need to spread conservative ideology. There was no self-interest on my part except for a desire to make piles and piles of money that was mine, all mine.

 @MontyWashburn But the big time comedy outlets - Breitbart, NRATV, Daily Stormer - all rejected the idea of financing a show for me. Admittedly, my work wasn't quite up to their high standards of racism and anti-semitism, but I am young and willing to learn and grow.

 @MontyWashburn So if I was to win over the elite of the anti-elitists, I had to make a bigger splash and then one day inspiration struck in the form of a homeless person who tried to bum money off of me.

 @MontyWashburn I wanted to yell, "get a Patreon, loser," but then I came up with a better idea that could potentially raise me some much needed funds.

 @MontyWashburn I conceived a project in which I would go around town and take money from homeless people.

 @MontyWashburn The squalor and despair of New York City was the perfect setting for the gentle whimsical humor I was attempting to find.

 @MontyWashburn The first street people I approached were a man and woman whose wardrobe was a little fancy, considering that they were obviously homeless and even more obviously black.

 @MontyWashburn Still, when I confronted them and tried to take their money, they got all indignant like I was the one being an asshole.

@MontyWashburn A wussy dude wearing an apron came over and told me they weren't homeless, and I said, well, then, why are they sitting outside, and he said, because this is an outdoor cafe.

 @MontyWashburn I didn't press the issue because the dude in the apron was way too white to be homeless, but he was just liberal enough to get a job waiting on black homeless people.

 @MontyWashburn I didn't believe this phony "outdoor cafe" story for one minute, but I did order a large coffee and a blueberry scone because I hadn't had breakfast, even though as a conservative I've always known that breakfast is the most important meal to deny poor people of the day.

 @MontyWashburn The afternoon wasn't all like this. I was able to capture on camera lots of footage of me making fun of many destitute people who smelled like pee, but as satisfying as this was, I wasn't raising much money for my own project.

 @MontyWashburn That's the trouble with homeless people - they're not good earners.

 @MontyWashburn But then it looked like my prospects were about to improve, I saw a homeless guy who looked a little healthier than the others.

 @MontyWashburn He was wearing a comfortable overcoat and had a well groomed handlebar mustache that made me wonder if vagrancy might be a spawning ground for the next generation of barbershop quartets.

 @MontyWashburn There was a bit of a disheveled nature to his appearance, but he was much more put together than the other homeless people. It was nice to finally run into a scummy street slime-ball who might actually be good at his job.

@MontyWashburn I approached him with my hidden camera and began ridiculing and denigrating his appearance with more respect than was my usual method.

 @MontyWashburn But he was having none of it. "Get away from me," he said. "I know who you are."

 @MontyWashburn At first I was flattered that he might be a fan, but then he said, "I have a hidden camera, too," and now I knew who he was: John Stossel, the consumer advocate who had made a name for himself advocating against consumers, first on ABC News, then on Fox.

 @MontyWashburn I immediately figured out that he was doing his own investigation into how awful homeless people were.

 @MontyWashburn I wasn't surprised that another right wing media personality was making fun of homeless people. It's one of those great ideas that's just out there in the conservative stream of consciousness.

 @MontyWashburn But Stossel was acting like I had wandered onto his turf. I could tell he was pissed, but I didn't want to get into a hassle with him, so I just grabbed his cup full of money and ran.

 @MontyWashburn That was the moment I found out that despite his dorky mustache, John Stossel is a good athlete.

 @MontyWashburn He tackled me on the sidewalk and as he pummeled me, a crowd gathered. He was recognized by a few passersby and he was able to sign autographs while he continued to repeatedly punch me. I had to admire his professionalism.

@MontyWashburn But he was angrier than ever. I had blown his cover and he had to postpone his homeless undercover investigation, which was scheduled to coincide with his week-long "Are Refugee Orphans Assholes?" investigative series.

 @MontyWashburn I had ruined his plans so he was treating me like a faulty driver-side airbag that he had an irrational grudge against.

 @MontyWashburn "Your career in Conservative media is over!" he screamed. I didn't know if he had the power to pull this off, but sure enough, I soon found that I was not welcome at Fox News.

 @MontyWashburn Not that I had ever been welcome there in the first place. I had done a couple of appearances, but the problems started when I was tested in front of focus groups.

 @MontyWashburn A producer pulled me aside to tell me the results. "You know how the camera loves some faces?" he said. "Well, the camera sends your face restraining orders."

 @MontyWashburn This was a surprise to me. Not to be vain, but I always thought that I had the looks of a movie star, especially after someone told me that I resembled the banjo playing kid from Deliverance.

 @MontyWashburn But the John Stossel incident cinched it: I was now officially banned at Fox News. Because I was deemed un-telegenic, I was now being discriminated against and thus denied the opportunity to discriminate against others. So unfair!

 @MontyWashburn My career was in trouble. For an ideology that ignores poverty and advocates the decimation of entire classes and races of people, conservatism can be surprisingly cruel sometimes.

@MontyWashburn I had to find something that would get me back in the game. And then, on a community bulletin board at the Club For Growth's website on the dark web, I saw that General Stone was planning a top secret commando operation and was looking for recruits.

 @MontyWashburn From what little I know about the mission, it seems as if it would be like taking candy from a baby.

 @MontyWashburn And since I had already tried to ingratiate myself to the right wing by making a series of videos where I actually took candy from babies (not as easy as they say, infants tend to be loud and dickish about it), this whole commando thing is certainly something worth pursuing.

The twitter timeline of Carol Connelly is also of value to this inquiry; and since she is the only woman on the commando team, the Republican Senators on this committee are advised to treat her as an equal in this investigation and save your impulse to deny her control over her own body for another time.

 @CarolConnelly I am Christian. I am Conservative. I have great hair. Yet I don't have my own show on a right wing cable news network. Why is this?

 @CarolConnelly Oh, I forgot to mention, I'm a woman.

 @CarolConnelly I guess it's God's will.

 @CarolConnelly And for all of His all-seeing, all-knowing ways, it appears that God does not watch basic cable. I would never under any circumstances say that God has forsaken me, but the television industry has forsaken me, and in my case, that might even be worse.

@CarolConnelly The Lord does indeed work in delirious ways.

 @CarolConnelly And I have never been one to question His judgement.

 @CarolConnelly But I still have to wonder why He saw fit to allow the conservative cable news media that it has always been my life's dream to work for to be run by a bunch of pompous pigs who would discard Satan's resume for not listing enough instances of evil.

 @CarolConnelly I'm tempted to call them the scum of the earth but scum was part of the earth that God created, so that would be giving them too much praise.

 @CarolConnelly And it's not that I wasn't qualified to work in conservative media.

 @CarolConnelly I have doctorate in communications from Bob Jones University.

 @CarolConnelly I assisted on the Mein Kampf For Kids series that the short-lived Breitbart, Jr network produced.

 @CarolConnelly I did a bunch of You Tube interviews with CPAC attendees that was quite informative, especially after I got them to speak up so they could be heard through their white hoods.

 @CarolConnelly No, I'm not blonde. I am as the Lord made me, a brunette, with hazel eyes, a pert face and a compact body that has stayed fit through the grace of God and a lack of carbs.

@CarolConnelly But I'm not blonde. Anti-Fake News organizations put a high premium on artificiality, and I was considering a baptismal ceremony involving peroxide, but then, saints be praised, there was a job opening and I scored an interview!

@CarolConnelly I had a meeting with Bob McGlory, who as you know was the number one news personality on the network. I was excited and intimidated to meet him.

@CarolConnelly I knew instinctively that he was a miserable piece of shit, but he was a miserable piece of shit who promoted an agenda I believed in, so God forgive me, I wanted to work with him.

@CarolConnelly And he was quite charming during our initial interview. He asked me a little bit about my life but mostly he talked about his favorite subject: himself.

@CarolConnelly He had streaks of grey that sat like jetties in a sea of black hair dye. In front of a camera his face was smooth and charismatic, but in person, you could see a facial line representing all 60 years of his life, even though he's only 55.

@CarolConnelly But it was his power that he wore like cologne, and it was meant to be an irresistible aphrodisiac, and I have to admit that indeed it was. To him.

@CarolConnelly At the time he had his finger on the pulse of American Conservatism, I just didn't know that he was soon going to have his finger on the pulse of his penis as he talked to me on the telephone.

@CarolConnelly But none of that mattered then because I was an employed person when I walked out of that office decorated with photoshopped pictures of McGlory with various celebrities.

@CarolConnelly At least I think they were photoshopped; I doubt if he ever really punched Gandhi in the face.

 @CarolConnelly It wasn't an on-air position, not yet anyway. I would have to work my way up through the ranks, starting with a behind-the-scenes assignment as a segment producer.

 @CarolConnelly Not my dream job, but it felt as if God had put me on the path towards my dream job. I know now that if God spoke to me directly He would say, "hey lady, don't associate me with that shit show," but at the time I was excited.

 @CarolConnelly By the way, I do use profanity a lot more than I used to, but I am not yet ready to ask for God's forgiveness because I wouldn't be surprised if the state of the world He created has resulted in our Lord and Savior putting coins in His curse jar every day.

 @CarolConnelly I showed up for work on that first Monday morning with a great attitude, ready to do whatever needed to be done.

 @CarolConnelly I was there to learn, so no assignment would be too small or demeaning for me. Things got small and demeaning real fast, but at first I was given a task that was quite important.

 @CarolConnelly I was handed the solemn responsibility of carrying the transcripts of the talking points the Republican National Committee sent over to our news room every day and then personally delivering them to Bob McGlory.

@CarolConnelly It's an essential task. The network prides itself on being at the forefront of breaking news, so whenever the RNC talking points arrived, it was with the utmost urgency that I took the readout to McGlory's office.

 @CarolConnelly Mr. McGlory seemed happy with the job I was doing, although the way he expressed it was by saying things like, "Nice blouse," "sexy dress" and "are those real?"

 @CarolConnelly I smiled and resisted the urge to kick him in the groin because I was on a career path, and I just had to accept that this particular path happened to be covered in dog shit.

 @CarolConnelly I had ambitions beyond my behind-the scenes role. I didn't want to just be the person putting words into the TelePrompTer, I wanted to be the person reading the words that were put into the TelePrompTer.

 @CarolConnelly I held out the hope that once I had established myself as a popular on-air personality, THEN I could start kneeing my male coworkers in the groin. It was a dream worth having.

 @CarolConnelly So I stayed humble, did my job, and waited for opportunity to knock. But unfortunately, at this network, opportunity doesn't knock, it calls you up on the phone and massages its ding-dong.

 @CarolConnelly Mr. McGlory was difficult to work with, but I kept telling myself that this was a temporary situation; only the emotional scars were permanent, and when the time came I would have my church, my therapist, and my pharmacist to deal with the inevitable PTSD.

@CarolConnelly I had to figure out how to handle this situation. As much as I yearned to learn everything this iconic media phenom could teach me, its hard to absorb the lessons of someone who is basically Porn Hub in a business suit.

 @CarolConnelly It is now well known that he used to call me up at night and touch himself in inappropriate ways while expressing scenarios that turned restaurant condiments and everyday bathroom products into objects of horror.

 @CarolConnelly I am aware that young women starting out in the workforce who work for older, powerful men suffer the same kind of masturba-mentoring that I went through, but that doesn't make it any easier to endure.

 @CarolConnelly As Mr. McGlory sat across from me behind his desk and went through each RNC talking point, he stroked his private parts (not nearly private enough as far as I was concerned) harder and harder depending on the policy being discussed.

 @CarolConnelly Cutting taxes for the rich got him off, so did denying healthcare to the poor, but any story about people of color made him lose his boner. Whenever there was a military tragedy he'd ask me to show proper respect by wearing my blouse at half mast.

 @CarolConnelly I'm proud to say that I did not take off any clothing, nor did I acquiesce to any of his more questionable requests (he tried to convince me that we'd understand a water rights bill better if we read it while taking a shower together, but I wasn't buying it.)

 @CarolConnelly I was on the verge of quitting, but then I purchased special contact lenses that enabled my eyes to look like they were open but were in fact closed. It was a desperate attempt to protect my vision from the human atrocity that unfolded before my eyes.

 @CarolConnelly The sad truth is that many women don't get far in the corporate world without a man in a more powerful position helping them. It's a case of one hand washing the other, except in this case it was only the hand of my boss that needed the washing.

 @CarolConnelly As long as I maintained a neutral expression while he grunted and contorted his face into a Picasso painting, everything seemed "normal," but the main trick was getting the contacts on and off before and after I entered the office.

 @CarolConnelly This was counterintuitive, because a good reporter is supposed to be observant of all things at all times and here I was doing everything I could to avert my eyes at all costs.

 @CarolConnelly Don't forget, for all intents and purposes, I was blind while I was wearing these lenses, so I certainly didn't want anyone to know this, especially considering that this was a work environment where making fun of disabled people was encouraged.

 @CarolConnelly So I had to finesse this circumstance with great care, but unfortunately, life is better at fucking you than most men are.

 @CarolConnelly Please, pardon my french, but I'm afraid that on this one misbegotten afternoon, the intersection of politics, religion and sex collided in a way that screwed me once and for all.

 @CarolConnelly On the afternoon in question, I wasn't able to remove my lenses until I got out of Mr. McGlory's office. Before my sight was restored, I bumped into Mike Pence — the Governor of Indiana at the time.

@CarolConnelly He was at the studio being interviewed to promote his initiative to prosecute homosexuals for ordering pizza online or something like that, I don't quite remember, it was several initiatives against homosexuals ago.

 @CarolConnelly The Governor and I made physical contact, and all hell broke loose, and by that I mean Pence literally reacted as if the floor opened up and the Devil himself emerged from the very bowels of Hades to see if it was okay to use the copy machine.

 @CarolConnelly "Get it off me! Get it off me!" he yelled, the "it" he was referring to was me.

 @CarolConnelly I got my blindness-inducing contacts out really quick and stepped back. The Governor was shaking and wiping his body as if it was covered by spiders.

 @CarolConnelly "Girl cooties! Girl cooties!" he screamed. Then he repeatedly called out, "Mommy! Mommy!" I knew that he was referring to his wife, who wasn't there at the time so now he was coming to the panicked realization that he had allowed himself to be in close proximity to a female.

 @CarolConnelly His handlers whisked him away. He still did the interview and was able to call for the discrimination of a large group of Americans without revealing to the home viewer his cootie-based trauma. Everyone at the network was impressed by his composure.

 @CarolConnelly I later found out that he took a shower in the CEO's office with all of his clothes still on. He wiped soap and water all over his suit while sitting on the floor in the fetal position and weeping uncontrollably.

@CarolConnelly And me, being a girl and all, was the culprit. I had accidentally touched a man, which in this corporate world was much more egregious than a man purposely and aggressively touching a woman.

 @CarolConnelly Of course, I was called into Mr. McGlory's office. I knew something was amiss when I saw that he wasn't jacking-off.

 @CarolConnelly "You've stepped over a line," he said, wiping his hand with a Kleenex purely out of habit.

 @CarolConnelly "But I didn't mean to..." I started to reply.

 @CarolConnelly "You violated the personal space of a major figure in a political party that we've given our non-partisan support to," he said. "He's a deeply religious man and as a woman, you violated his spiritual beliefs by allowing yourself to get in his line of sight."

 @CarolConnelly I didn't know what to say. My only goal in life was to be a conservative broadcaster but I hadn't known when I started out that the major downside to this was having to spend time around conservative broadcasters.

 @CarolConnelly Finally I said, "What can I do? How can I make this right?"

 @CarolConnelly He sighed, but there was a sympathetic cadence to it, like a dissonant song with some melodic content.

 @CarolConnelly I'd be lying if I said I wasn't expecting what came next.

 @CarolConnelly "If you let me tea-bag you, we can put this all behind us," he said.

@CarolConnelly I picked up a stapler and threw it at his head. It hit him hard and he fell to the floor. This action was certainly not in line with my Christian beliefs. So why did it feel so good?

 @CarolConnelly I assumed I had killed him. In that instant, I saw my whole life flash before my eyes, and that was really distressing because it meant I had to watch him masturbate again.

 @CarolConnelly But he wasn't dead. He was shaken and discombobulated, but to my great relief he was still alive. I'd always known that office supplies don't kill people, people kill people, and I was relieved that as of yet I was not a killer.

 @CarolConnelly Then, when he rose to his feet, it seemed to me that I was even in more trouble than if I had actually finished him off. He was drooling and babbling incoherently, saying things like, "No, papa don't hurt me!" and "I will never disappoint you, papa!"

 @CarolConnelly Now I felt like I was in the biggest kind of trouble imaginable. I had tossed a metal object at the head of the most powerful and popular cable news anchor in the world and had caused what appeared to be irreparable brain damage.

 @CarolConnelly He was having a psychotic break which was making him think I was his father. So I had achieved the impossible - I made him weirder than he already was.

 @CarolConnelly Then another producer entered the office. He asked McGlory about a programming decision and he replied something along the lines of, "We'll open with the welfare cheat story, then segue to sanctuary cities and close with HOW DARE YOU IMPLY MY FATHER NEVER LOVED ME!!!"

@CarolConnelly The producer, who apparently was used to this sort of thing, just said, "Got it, boss, will do." Then he smiled affably and exited the room.

 @CarolConnelly In fact, the responses Mr. McGlory gave in the wake of this incident were considered perfectly normal by everyone and the ratings and profits for the channel only grew. The entire news network was only one serious brain injury away from true success.

 @CarolConnelly McGlory didn't fire me or even reprimand me over this. For once his damaged mind was working in my favor.

 @CarolConnelly Except it wasn't. I was still in the same miserable mess. McGlory recovered from the stapler injury and snapped back to his old coherent loathsomeness. He resumed phoning me at home.

 @CarolConnelly Not long after, I sued his ass for sexual harassment. What happened in the office was of less consequence; it was the phone calls that brought him down because of a simple device he apparently wasn't aware of called a tape recorder.

 @CarolConnelly But that was all in the future. At that moment I just wanted to get as far away from everyone and everything as possible. The Three Mile Island-level of toxic masculinity in this work environment had driven me to a violent use of office supplies.

 @CarolConnelly Soon I was out of a job, and the settlement from a lawsuit was at that time just a hypothetical gleam in my traumatized eyes. I didn't see a future for me in the TV News business.

 @CarolConnelly But then something unexpected happened. The liberal cable news network, located just across sixth avenue from our conservative cable news network, contacted me about coming in to meet with them.

@CarolConnelly I really didn't believe in their philosophy of liberalism, but a job is a job is a job. (I realize I'm paraphrasing a radical lesbian here, but desperate times call for desperate quotations.)

 @CarolConnelly So I agreed to come in for the interview but I did have trepidation about this network. Only about seventy percent of their programming is conservative so they are an extremist liberal progressive channel. That kind of radicalism gives me pause.

 @CarolConnelly But when I arrived at the offices, I was impressed that none of the men appeared to be whacking off. This was a novel approach to corporate culture that I was at least willing to give a chance.

 @CarolConnelly I met with the head of the network, an efficient generator of automatic affability with a shiny bald head and an even shinier Armani suit.

 @CarolConnelly "We want our channel to have a diverse point of view," he said. "Despite our reputation, we do feature right wing voices, but we'd like to mix things up and contrast that with extreme right wing voices."

 @CarolConnelly That sounded reasonable, but the stark fact was that the network featured many moderate Republicans, so there was no denying that it was liberal.

 @CarolConnelly I knew that his interest in me was mainly based on my notoriety, but the offer he made felt like God opening a door. Would I want to be the fill-in host of their flagship morning show?

 @CarolConnelly The host was once a Republican congressman who had been instrumental in the impeachment of Bill Clinton.

@CarolConnelly This had happened a few marriages and many infidelities ago.

 @CarolConnelly But now he was married to his female cohost, who was the daughter of a Carter Administration official, so her background in radical Marxist ideology had obviously had an influence on her cohost/husband.

 @CarolConnelly You didn't always agree with them, but you had to admit that his passive/aggressive berating of her made for compelling television. It was like watching a three hour production of Who's Afraid of Virginia Wolfe every morning.

 @CarolConnelly But was I up to the challenge of filling in for her every now and then?

 @CarolConnelly I wasn't sure, but I was willing to give it a try. Opportunity was knocking, I just had to hope it wouldn't knock me to the ground and rob me of my dignity like it did at the other channel.

 @CarolConnelly Once I showed up at work, it was immediately apparent that the environment at the liberal channel was different than it had been at the conservative channel.

 @CarolConnelly The communistic atmosphere fostered an attitude than any man, no matter his station in life, was capable of getting paid more than a woman.

 @CarolConnelly Some of the men were quite gentlemanly in the way they made a point of removing the porn sites they were watching on computer consoles as I walked past their cubicles.

 @CarolConnelly But I wasn't there to socialize with socialists.

@CarolConnelly I wanted to focus on my work and make a name for myself. I realized that many conservative viewers would be upset that I was associating with people who were slightly less conservative than some other conservatives.

 @CarolConnelly But I had no interest in preaching to the choir, especially since many in that choir wouldn't listen to a female preacher anyway.

 @CarolConnelly My first morning when I guest hosted on the show, I was welcomed warmly by the host and his panel, which consisted of four of the highest paid pundits in the media.

 @CarolConnelly These pontificators (all men) were so successful they had achieved that rarified place in journalism where they never had to do any actual journalism anymore.

 @CarolConnelly Their only job was to act as protectors of conventional wisdom, which they guarded like Secret Service agents who never shut up.

 @CarolConnelly Conventional Wisdom was a sacred scroll that was never to be altered lest their world of access and privilege perish from this earth.

 @CarolConnelly I was only too happy to be part of this agenda. As I sat on the panel that first morning, I was more than ready to add my voice to the chorus of conformity that helped the rich and powerful start their day.

 @CarolConnelly But I didn't have the kind of interaction with the other panelists that I was hoping for.

 @CarolConnelly Whenever I offered an opinion, always with a big, affable I'm-a-girl-but-I'm-cool-about-stuff smile, the men on the panel reacted with sneers, snickers, and elbowing among themselves, as if condescension was a Peabody Award category.

 @CarolConnelly I soon realized that I was only there to give them something to feel superior to. This should have made me feel like an accepted member of the populace, since they felt superior to everyone, but it had the opposite effect on me.

 @CarolConnelly For instance, when I gave my opinion on an economic issue, one of the other pundits brought up the important issue of how his wife can't balance a check book, to much laughter from the other guys.

 @CarolConnelly I didn't get into this business for prizes, but at that moment I was certain our show was a shoo-in for best newscast of 1962.

 @CarolConnelly I am a big believer in a strong national defense, but when the President threatened to go to war and I used the word, "frightening" instead of the preferred word, "presidential," the other panelists mocked me for being a snowflake.

 @CarolConnelly I was being disrespected, which as a woman in the TV news business meant I had arrived.

 @CarolConnelly There are only a handful of opportunities for a woman to be humiliated on national television, and a part of me knew that I should be grateful that I was one of the chosen few.

 @CarolConnelly But there was another part of me that was fed up with all the toxic masculinity and all I could think was, "oh, fuck this."

 @CarolConnelly Well, actually, as you might already know, I didn't just think this, I said it out loud. In the middle of some testosterone reverie by the other panelists, I blurted out "oh, fuck this" on morning television.

42

@CarolConnelly It went viral, and this wasn't just some instant internet phenomenon that came and went, the controversy lasted a whole day. I was certainly more famous than ever, but my career as a broadcast journalist was effectively over.

 @CarolConnelly I shouldn't have done it. My religious upbringing taught me that my role as a woman was to serve men. But as far as I'm concerned, that spiritual belief is null and void until men stop behaving like jerks, so in other words, till the end of time.

 @CarolConnelly Jesus was a man, this I do not dispute. But there is nothing ungodly about thinking that men are assholes. I mean, look at what a bunch of assholes they were towards Jesus when he was alive!

 @CarolConnelly My experience in the media world had messed with my head to the point that a Tourette's-like reaction had caused me to utter a vulgarity on national television.

 @CarolConnelly Well, shit happens.

 @CarolConnelly I had performed an act of disrespect deemed unacceptable by the male powers that be. It's odd that an industry filled with chronic masturbators doesn't like being told to go fuck itself, but there you have it.

 @CarolConnelly So once again, I was out of work, and this time without job prospects. What was I going to do?

 @CarolConnelly I didn't know.

@CarolConnelly But I just heard about General Stone's covert commando mission. It was discussed on Megyn Kelly's show this morning, so clearly they're serious about keeping it top secret. I'm going to look into this.

PART TWO

Although the individual Twitter timelines have been of use to this committee, once the subjects of our investigation began interacting with each other, much more was revealed about the nature of this endeavor.

The following is General Stone's initial exchange with Bob McGlory.

@GeneralStone When I started putting together my team for this mission, you were the first person I thought of, McGlory. I know that you are out of work and looking for something to do.

 @BobMcGlory Out of work? Looking for something to do? You are aware that I am doing a podcast, right?

 @GeneralStone Yes, of course! I listen to it every week.

 @BobMcGlory It's on every day! I do it from my big empty Westchester mansion every afternoon. It's awesome! I'm having the time of my my life.

 @GeneralStone Well, then I won't bother you.

 @BobMcGlory No, wait, don't log off, speak to me. I am open to hearing your plan.

 @GeneralStone Okay, pay strict attention, because I am aware that you will have to carefully weigh your options before you decide.

 @BobMcGlory I'll do it!

 @GeneralStone But I haven't told you what it is yet.

 @BobMcGlory Of course, I'll need to know the details before I decide anything.

@GeneralStone Yes, that's perfectly understandable.

 @BobMcGlory I'll do it!

 @GeneralStone But your podcast.

 @BobMcGlory I said I'll do it. It's a military operation, right?

 @GeneralStone Yes, although I know you don't have a strong military background.

 @BobMcGlory What? Are you kidding? I may not have ever been in the military per say, but as a war correspondent, I was in the shit, man!

 @GeneralStone In the Falkland Islands?

 @BobMcGlory Yes! The room service in the hotel just across the ocean from the skirmish was crap, and the liberal news network that I worked for at the time wouldn't cover the mini-bar in my expense account. I still sometimes wake up in the middle of the night, screaming.

 @GeneralStone But you covered the conflict, right?

@BobMcGlory Of course I did! As a reporter, I am always the first one on the scene when someone is ready to give a second hand account.

 @GeneralStone Okay, but this mission is going to involve real danger. We are going to explode a stink bomb in a large chateau filled with top level liberals. If we succeed, we will once again be the heroes of conservatism we deserve to be.

 @BobMcGlory I already am a hero of conservatism.

 @GeneralStone Yes, but you've been banned from conservative media. This will change that.

 @BobMcGlory Then let's do it!

 @GeneralStone Okay, but keep in mind, if we fail, we'll be ostracized by people we never respected in the first place. Are you sure you are willing to take that kind of risk?

 @BobMcGlory You'd better believe I am! America will never be truly great until I'm making $28 million a year again.

 @GeneralStone Your passion for your country is just what we need on this mission. But I should point out that it will also be dangerous. Physically dangerous.

 @BobMcGlory Ha! I laugh in the face of danger! And it's real laughter, not the fake kind of laughter I gave when Dennis Miller used to be on my show.

@GeneralStone That's good to know, but I just want to be clear that this mission will require courage. Physical courage.

 @BobMcGlory Not a problem. I have just one question.

 @GeneralStone What's that?

 @BobMcGlory Can I hire a flunky to do all the dangerous stuff for me?

 @GeneralStone No, but just remember, if we complete this mission successfully, you'll once again be in a position to exploit vulnerable, low-level employees.

 @BobMcGlory Hearing that, I just felt a chill up my leg.

 @GeneralStone In the meantime, check out www.stinkbombs.com on the dark web. They have exactly the kind of destructive weaponry we're looking for, plus some really fun emojis.

 @BobMcGlory Now that I'm not going into the office every day, I spend a lot of time on the dark web. It's great! The Neo-Nazi sites there are much more stylish than the ones on the regular web.

 @GeneralStone Listen, just for the sake of appearances, are you sure it's a good idea to visit those sites?

@BobMcGlory I just like to see what my fans are up to.

 @GeneralStone Fair enough, but we need to stay focused on the task at hand.

 @BobMcGlory Agreed. One more question.

 @GeneralStone Okay.

 @BobMcGlory Who owns the exclusive rights to this commando raid? What will my percentage be if the carnage we cause goes into syndication?

 @GeneralStone Not sure if this type of mission has much of an afterlife in syndication, but there might be some ancillary markets we can exploit. Plus, we'll be helping to create a brave new world of conservative cultural dominance, and that will mean big bucks for us.

 @BobMcGlory Well I would think so! Conservatism without big bucks might as well be liberalism.

 @GeneralStone Fair point. Now I've got to ask - what experience do you have with explosives?

 @BobMcGlory Plenty of experience.

@GeneralStone For instance?

 @BobMcGlory Well, I have a first hand familiarity with David Niven in The Guns of Navarone.

 @GeneralStone That's a movie. Not sure it counts

 @BobMcGlory You're missing my point. When I was covering the invasion of Iraq, the Guns Of Navarone was playing in the Four Seasons Hotel I was staying at.

 @GeneralStone The Four Seasons hotel you stayed in during the invasion? In Iraq?

 @BobMcGlory Well, I was all set to go to Iraq, right at the start of the invasion. God, that was a great time to be alive.

 @GeneralStone I know. That war was my big career break.

 @BobMcGlory Yeah, anyway, I was on my way, and there was nothing more important to me than being on the front lines of action. But then I got word that Chuck Woolery wanted me to be a guest on his syndicated talk show.

 @GeneralStone Chuck Woolery had a talk show?

@BobMcGlory Yes, but the mainstream media conspired to keep it a secret after it tanked in the ratings and got cancelled.

 @GeneralStone That makes me so mad.

 @BobMcGlory I know, right? Anyway, instead of going to Iraq, I went to Los Angeles to do Chuck's show.

 @GeneralStone Really?

 @BobMcGlory Yes, and I've never regretted the decision.

 @GeneralStone Why would you?

 @BobMcGlory And I still managed to cover the war! I was able to give exclusive, on the scene reports based on what I was seeing on CNN in my hotel room.

 @GeneralStone I remember watching! I must say, your reporting on CNN's reporting was so much better than CNN's reporting. But what does this have to do with your knowledge of explosives?

 @BobMcGlory Well, the cable system in the Four Seasons Hotel in LA also had Turner Classic Movies, and they were showing an entire evening of Irene Papas films. But being the keen reporter I was, I ascertained that the real story was David Niven, and possibly Anthony Quayle. And that's how I know about explosives.

@GeneralStone You're on medication, aren't you?

 @BobMcGlory Always.

 @GeneralStone Glad we got that cleared up. Now that you're on board, it's time to get the rest of the team together.

 @BobMcGlory Wait a minute, did you say, rest of the team?

 @GeneralStone Yes, I told you this was a commando TEAM I'm starting.

 @BobMcGlory But I was the first one you picked, right?

 @GeneralStone Of course.

 @BobMcGlory Good. I was number one in cable news so I expect to be number one in commando teams.

 @GeneralStone You certainly are.

 @BobMcGlory Okay, but let all the others know that I have one condition if I'm to anchor this team.

@GeneralStone What's that?

 @BobMcGlory No egos.

General Stone was then contacted by Monty Washburn. Here is the transcript of their thread.

 @GeneralStone I appreciate your interest in this mission, Monty, so I don't want to be negative, but you seem like kind of a dipshit.

 @MontyWashburn General, I've been called a dipshit my whole life, but if I don't speak for the dipshits of the world, who will?

 @GeneralStone That's a noble sentiment, but it doesn't mean you can necessarily handle a highly dangerous mission of this sort.

 @MontyWashburn I'm honored, it's great to be on board, General.

 @GeneralStone You're not on board, son. I'll be honest, your history of being an asshole is a mark against you.

 @MontyWashburn Sir, with all due respect, I may be an asshole, but I'm your kind of asshole.

 @GeneralStone No, you are not. My kind of asshole is the strong, military kind. But you're the weak, weaselly kind.

@MontyWashburn Fair enough, but General, let me ask, can you imagine anyone being intimidated by me?

 @GeneralStone Absolutely not.

 @MontyWashburn Can you picture anyone ever being threatened by me?

 @GeneralStone Hell no!

 @MontyWashburn I agree. And it means no one in this liberal Aspen enclave will see me coming.

 @GeneralStone So, you're saying that you are so stupid, so incompetent, so downright dipshitty that people's guards will be down?

 @MontyWashburn General, I am humbled that you get me, you really get me!

 @GeneralStone Actually, I don't. I really don't. Look, it's been nice talking to you.

 @MontyWashburn I beg you, General, please give me a chance!

 @GeneralStone But what exactly can you bring to the table?

@MontyWashburn If that table is covered with bowls of Grey Poupon mustard, I can bring laxative. And if I put that laxative into the bowls of mustard, it may just give you the edge you need.

 @GeneralStone What experience do you have in covert digestion subversion?

 @MontyWashburn Sir, covertly inducing diarrhea is exactly the kind of black-opps I am good at. I once slipped ex-lax into the entire Jamba Juice order of an Occupy Wall Street protest in lower Manhattan.

 @MontyWashburn By the time I was through, the only thing that was occupied was every porto-potty in Battery Park!

 @GeneralStone It's quite admirable that you pulled it off. But can you achieve the same effect on a larger scale?

 @MontyWashburn Sir, after I'm done, I'll turn every bleeding heart liberal into a shitting ass liberal.

 @GeneralStone Son, you're making a convincing case for yourself. I never heard anyone talk so enthusiastically about making other people shit their pants.

 @MontyWashburn So I'm on the mission?

 @GeneralStone Yes, God help me. You're on the mission.

 @MontyWashburn General, I just want to say what an honor this is and that you have my word that I will never, ever let you down.

@GeneralStone Fine. Be ready at 0:200 hours tomorrow for a briefing.

 @MontyWashburn I can't. I have a thing.

 @GeneralStone Oh, for Christ's sake!

The next addition to this commando team was a surprise, especially considering her history with Bob McGlory. The twitter conversation she had with General Stone is presented here to the committee.

 @CarolConnelly I heard about your mission, General. I think it's something I might want to be a part of.

 @GeneralStone I do have some concerns about your presence on the team.

 @CarolConnelly I hope it's not because I'm a woman. I can handle myself as well as any man.

 @GeneralStone That is adorable, but there's something about this operation you might want to know.

 @CarolConnelly Look, if there's one thing I am certain of, it's that I need to be part of something new. I alienated a lot of conservatives when I appeared on that slightly less conservative network. In order to win them back, I need to piss off liberals.

 @GeneralStone But aren't conservatives happy that you upset your liberal cohosts?

@CarolConnelly I got a lot of blowback from the Christian community. They don't like that I expressed a profanity.

 @GeneralStone You'd like to redeem yourself in their eyes?

 @CarolConnelly Fuck no. But I want my career back. I've prayed and looked deep into my soul and realized that I need to do something that will get me back on television. I see the light of the Lord in the red light of a TV camera.

 @GeneralStone Are you one of those Conservative Christians who can only bask in the glow of God's love if liberals are suffering?

 @CarolConnelly As beautiful as that sentiment is, if I'm honest with myself, I have to say that I don't take pleasure in anyone's suffering.

 @GeneralStone Then I'm not sure you're right for this mission. And I've buried the lede. I haven't told you the aspect of this team-up that is most pertinent to you.

 @CarolConnelly I don't envision there being any dealbreaker.

 @GeneralStone Bob McGlory is on this mission.

 @CarolConnelly That's a deal breaker.

 @GeneralStone I thought so.

@CarolConnelly No, wait a minute. Why should he get to go on this mission and not me?

 @GeneralStone Wait, before you jump to conclusions, and start yelling "sexism!" let me explain my reasons for thinking he can do the job and you can't.

 @CarolConnelly I'm listening.

 @GeneralStone He's a man and you're a woman.

 @CarolConnelly Well, that is certainly a nuanced hot take.

 @GeneralStone Look, I've always supported women in the military. My feeling was that the more women that go into battle, the less likely it meant that I'd have to.

 @CarolConnelly How very woke of you.

 @GeneralStone But come on, if you join this mission, you'll have to work with Bob McGlory. You sued him for sexual harassment. That's going to be an awkward situation to say the least.

 @CarolConnelly You make a good point. Plus I don't want to be around that asshat.

 @GeneralStone And like all women, especially attractive women, you'll be a huge distraction.

@CarolConnelly What? Excuse me?

 @GeneralStone Wait, don't take umbrage! I complimented you. I called you attractive. And I think women should be included in all workplace situations. Except important ones.

 @CarolConnelly Okay, I was ready to walk away, but now I'm going to insist that I be on this mission!

 @GeneralStone But I already told you: you're going to be a huge distraction!

 @CarolConnelly Exactly! That's why you need me.

 @GeneralStone What do you mean?

 @CarolConnelly Just what I said. I will be a distraction. My role in the mission will be to distract and misdirect the liberal men at the Aspen chateau while the rest of the team goes about their business.

 @GeneralStone I'm listening.

 @CarolConnelly In a way, I already went undercover with the liberals when I guest hosted that morning show. They know me. I've trained myself to actually look interested while they throw around words like "oligarchy" and "triangulation."

@GeneralStone That is quite a skill.

 @CarolConnelly Just moments ago, I even used the term "woke." I speak these people's language.

 @GeneralStone I admit, this could be a valuable skill on this mission.

 @CarolConnelly Yes. I can manipulate their innate liberalism to the point where they become consumed with paralyzing self-loathing.

 @GeneralStone Really?

 @CarolConnelly Yes, that's why liberals like me.

 @GeneralStone Okay, I'm gonna take a risk and add you to our team. But that still begs the question: can you work with your arch-nemesis Bob McGlory?

 @CarolConnelly He's everybody's arch-nemesis.

 @GeneralStone That's not the point. And I have to tell you, this commando mission does not have the budget for a Human Resources Department.

 @CarolConnelly Don't worry. I know how to handle Bob McGlory.

@GeneralStone Okay, but just try not get any of your cooties on him.

 @CarolConnelly Wow, I have to say, this has degenerated into an incredibly immature conversation.

 @GeneralStone It feels good to be around conservatives again, doesn't it? Welcome onboard!

PART THREE

At this point, the full team was assembled - General Stone, Bob McGlory, Carol Connelly, and Monty Washburn. This was a TOP SECRET mission, so discretion was paramount, and communications would have to be covert and hidden from public scrutiny.

But they conversed via Twitter, which somewhat undermined this concept.

A record of their interactions is hereby submitted to the committee.

@GeneralStone The main thing we have to do is focus on the mission, and not be distracted by interpersonal disputes. Carol, I hope you can put the memory of Bob stroking his penis in front of you behind you.

 @CarolConnelly I'm ready to move forward with the utmost professionalism and only the greater good in mind.

 @BobMcGlory You see what a hysterical bitch she is?!!! No freaking way am I working with this woman!

 @CarolConnelly What's the matter, Bob? You don't have a problem working with women, do you?

 @BobMcGlory I work great with women, and I worked great with you! But you refused my mentoring.

 @CarolConnelly Mentoring? You made me listen while you rubbed tahini sauce on your genitals!

 @BobMcGlory And you learned nothing! You could have graduated from my segment producer to my mistress but you refused to grow as a person.

 @GeneralStone Okay, look, we can't let this petty squabbling distract us from our purpose. Can you both please just learn to have some mutual respect?

 @BobMcGlory General, that is a horrible thing to say. I am leaving this mission!

@CarolConnelly Good! I'll take all the credit and get the career boost in conservative media. You just stay in your basement and stick to your pathetic podcast.

 @BobMcGlory I happen to do my podcast in my dining room, with professional looking microphones and foam insulation! I even wear headphones, so suck on that!

 @CarolConnelly Sounds great. Why don't you return there right now? You need to be loyal to your listenership, both of them!

 @BobMcGlory On no you don't! You're not going to use your feminine wiles to get me to leave this mission, no way!

 @GeneralStone So you're staying on the mission?

 @BobMcGlory Yes! And for an important reason that's bigger than myself. I'm staying out of spite.

 @GeneralStone Great, nobody is leaving this mission, so let's go over the plan. Bob, did you acquire the explosives?

 @BobMcGlory They were delivered to my Westchester estate yesterday.

 @GeneralStone I hope the delivery was done in the utmost secrecy.

 @BobMcGlory Well, the delivery men arrived in the middle of my podcast, so I had them come on the show as guests.

@CarolConnelly So it was done in secret.

 @GeneralStone Bob, you shouldn't have done that! This commando mission is covert!

 @BobMcGlory General, I can assure you that any top secret information given out on my podcast is for premium subscribers only!

 @GeneralStone Well, as long as the bombs arrived, I think we can overlook any ill-advised podcasting that might have taken place.

 @BobMcGlory Oh, and by the way, I decided to go with a different bomb company than the one you recommended.

 @GeneralStone But this company has a very specific type of explosive that we have to use.

 @BobMcGlory Don't worry, I checked, they have the same exact kind of bomb in stock.

 @GeneralStone Fine, as long as they understand the highly classified nature of this endeavor.

 @BobMcGlory They do! They totally do! But in exchange for a discount on our explosives, they want us to promote their brand.

 @GeneralStone We can't promote brands. It's TOP SECRET.

@BobMcGlory I get it, but I don't see how a little product placement can hurt.

 @GeneralStone You're getting ahead of yourself. If this mission goes the way it's supposed to, they'll be plenty of business opportunities for all of us.

 @MontyWashburn This mission is already a great opportunity for me. I get to spike the mustard bowls with laxatives. I've been waiting all my life for an epic pranking opportunity like this.

 @BobMcGlory Say, you're a funny guy supposedly. Why don't you come up with a laxative-related joke?

 @MontyWashburn Oh, of course.

 @BobMcGlory Well, we're waiting.

 @MontyWashburn Uh, I'm trying to think of something. Give me a minute.

 @BobMcGlory Just forget about it.

 @MontyWashburn Wait, I've got it! Here it is - the laxatives are sure to make people have a desperate need to go to the bathroom! Ha, ha, LOL.

 @BobMcGlory What the fuck?

@GeneralStone That "joke" was neither L, O or L. Just stay focused on your part of the mission. Spiking the bowl with ex-lax is one thing, but the tricky part will be getting into the event.

 @MontyWashburn Don't worry, I have a great disguise that's sure to win first prize.

 @GeneralStone First prize? What are you talking about?

 @MontyWashburn Doesn't the event we're crashing have a cos-play contest?

 @GeneralStone I don't even know what that is.

 @MontyWashburn You said we needed disguises for this mission, right?

 @GeneralStone I did.

 @MontyWashburn Well, what is a disguise but cos-play? I've done cos-play at comic-cons.

 @BobMcGlory Comic-cons? That is pathetic. Aren't those comic book geeks a bunch of liberal loons?

 @MontyWashburn Not all of them. You'd be surprised, but the onslaught of female-driven Stars Wars movies and ethnicity diverse Superhero films has awakened the political consciousness of lonely fan boys everywhere.

@BobMcGlory "Fan Boys?" That sounds gay.

 @MontyWashburn Quite the opposite. Gay people tend to have a lot of sex, so they're nothing like fan boys at all.

 @BobMcGlory They don't get laid?

 @MontyWashburn I wouldn't put it that way. It's more that they never have sex. But they haven't taken the reluctance of women to lie down with them lying down.

 @CarolConnelly I have a bad feeling about where this conversation is heading.

 @MontyWashburn I'm just saying that certain comic book geeks have taken their sexual frustration and used it productively.

 @CarolConnelly How so?

 @MontyWashburn By harnessing that frustration and transforming it into hostility towards movies and TV shows that feature strong female protagonists.

 @BobMcGlory Gotta admit, these millennials might be more on the ball than I thought.

 @CarolConnelly Hey, here's an idea for comic-con cosplay: how about dressing up a a moral man who treats women respectfully.

 @MontyWashburn I'm into fantasy role play, but that's too far-out even for me. However, I figured that this commando mission, with its disguises and all, might be my first chance to win a cos-play pageant.

@GeneralStone We may be wearing disguises, but this ain't make-believe. It's the real thing.

 @MontyWashburn What kind of disguise will you be wearing?

 @GeneralStone I won't need one. I have been invited to come as myself to the event. I wrangled an invitation from Orville Pantalomur, the chairman of the Moderate Democrat Equivocators League.

 @BobMcGlory I used to have that guy on my show to represent the liberal point of view. I hate to praise a Democrat but I have to admit that I've never met anyone better at losing arguments.

 @GeneralStone Yes, I was on many pundit panels with him. He believes that the Democratic Party can only survive by never taking a stand on anything.

 @BobMcGlory One time on my show, after he said, "let's agree to disagree," he apologized for being too incendiary.

 @CarolConnelly He asked me out once, but before I could answer, he said, "Let's wait to hear what the people decide," then he ran out of the studio in a state of terror. I only wish most dudes were as gentlemanly.

 @MontyWashburn Would you have gone out with him?

 @CarolConnelly There was something sweet about his demeanor. The bow tie, the horn-rimmed glasses, the sense that not a hair was out of place even though he was bald. I don't think I'd ever get serious, but I could imagine grabbing coffee with him.

@BobMcGlory Whore.

 @CarolConnelly Asshole says what?

 @GeneralStone Come on, you two. Let's not allow this to degenerate into a situation where we are being completely honest with each other.

 @BobMcGlory Okay, but General, I'm curious, how come Orville Pantalomur invited you? You're as unwelcome in the world of mainstream politics as I am.

 @GeneralStone Well, I asked for an invitation and he and the other members of the Moderate Democrat Equivocators League all refused to take a stand on whether I should get one or not.

 @BobMcGlory Wimps! They're a disgrace to the principles they refuse to tell anyone they believe in.

 @GeneralStone After much tortured Hamlet-like deliberation, Orville said he'd be proud to have me as a guest, as long as his invitation was off the record.

 @CarolConnelly Sounds like going to the party means you have to hang out with the Democratic Equivocators League. How can that possibly be worth it?

 @GeneralStone Actually, I think It can work to our advantage. I will put them on the spot and pressure them into offering unvarnished opinions. The panicked equivocating will almost certainly cause a commotion that could provide us with cover.

@BobMcGlory Democrats are such pussies! I never equivocate! When I had my show, I always decided my political beliefs the minute RNC memos telling me what to believe arrived on my desk. It's called integrity.

 @GeneralStone I can go to the event as myself, but you can't, Bob. You'll have to go there undercover.

 @BobMcGlory That is certainly true. I mean, let's face it, I'm the most famous one here.

 @MontyWashburn So true. I've always admired how famous you are.

 @BobMcGlory My vast fame is another underreported story in the media.

 @MontyWashburn My goal is to be you one day.

 @CarolConnelly Of course. How could you not want Bob McGlory's life? The fame. The fortune. The abused ex-wife. The estranged, damaged children. The lack of any real friendship. The lonely, isolated existence in a gated estate.

 @BobMcGlory Hey, honey, stop trying to butter me up, I'm still pissed at you.

 @CarolConnelly I'm just pointing out that you live a life of quiet desperation.

 @BobMcGlory Not for long, baby! Before you know it, I'm going to go back to living a life of loud desperation!

@GeneralStone Let's all calm down. If this mission is to succeed, we all need to get along, and that requires cooperation.

 @BobMcGlory I am more than capable of cooperation, as long as everyone leaves me alone and let's me do whatever I want whenever I want.

 @GeneralStone Okay, but let's please just keep our eyes on the ball. This is a time for action, not introspection.

 @MontyWashburn I agree. The futility of introspection is something I've thought about a lot. But right now I want to tell you about my great disguise!

 @GeneralStone Are you going undercover as a non-dweeb?

 @MontyWashburn Exactly! I will disguise myself as George Clooney!

 @GeneralStone You look nothing like him.

 @MontyWashburn I promise you, if there are any "Facts of Life" fans at this party, they are going to be excited beyond belief!

 @GeneralStone You're talking about this mission like it's fun and games. It's not! Don't forget you have a grave and solemn responsibility — dousing the condiment bowl with laxatives.

 @MontyWashburn Don't worry, I guarantee you - those liberals will be shitting their pants so much they'll be shitting their pants.

@GeneralStone I don't know what you're saying, just get the job done. If all goes according to plan, McGlory, disguised as a janitor, will have planted the bombs by the time the panicked partygoers rush to the bathroom.

 @BobMcGlory Okay, but even if the laxative thing works, there will be partygoers who won't be eating the mustard.

 @GeneralStone That's where Carol and I come in. I will see to it that anyone who isn't running because of the laxative will be running away from the Moderate Democrat Equivocators League.

 @CarolConnelly And in the meantime, I will be engaging the people behind the new Grey Poupon upgrade with gushing praise about their artistry. They'll be so stuffed from me feeding their egos that they'll need to empty their bowels anyway.

 @GeneralStone The entire party will be a shambles, and the dearth of a Grey Poupon upgrade will be a major setback for liberalism in the United States.

 @MontyWashburn I'm so honored to be part of this mission and not some silly and stupid plan.

PART FOUR

The four members of the team continued their correspondence as they traveled from New York to Aspen. The decision to keep communicating with each other via Twitter was a fortuitous one for this committee however dumb it might have been for this group of newly minted commandoes.

@GeneralStone Okay, the Aspen Grey Poupon Point 2.0 Presentation Event is in a few days and we're on our way!

 @BobMcGlory Why aren't we flying first class? I love putting that hot towel on my dick.

 @GeneralStone You cannot bring explosives onto the plane.

 @BobMcGlory Even in first class?

 @GeneralStone No, not even there

 @BobMcGlory Damn intrusive government!

 @GeneralStone I think renting this limo and going all together to Aspen is the best solution.

 @MontyWashburn I know, right? Road Trip! Whoo Hoo!

 @BobMcGlory Don't you ever say or type or tweet the words Whoo or Hoo in my presence ever again, you millennial twerp!

 @CarolConnelly Hey, I'm a millennial.

 @BobMcGlory I don't mind it when a chick's a millennial. That's almost just the right age for me.

@CarolConnelly That's a pretty creepy thing to say, Bob. But maybe not by your standards. After all, I did once have to watch you have sex with a manilla envelope.

 @BobMcGlory I recycled it! But do liberals ever give me credit for anything? No!

 @GeneralStone Please let's stop this conversation right now and concentrate on the mission. We're on a two thousand mile road trip. So we all have to get along.

 @BobMcGlory Okay, but if we're all in the same limo, how come we're only communicating via social media?

 @GeneralStone I want this entire mission live-tweeted. As conservatives, we need to win over the young people. They don't think anything is real unless it's on the internet, so we need to keep up.

 @BobMcGlory I am very much in tune with modern technology, which I pointed out in the Western Union telegram I sent you last week.

 @GeneralStone I just want us to stay focused and not get bogged down in bickering.

 @BobMcGlory I agree, and guess what, I've got a great way to pass the time on this trip: I brought the entire collection of my books on tape that we can all listen to.

 @CarolConnelly Great! (I'm not sure if I am properly conveying my sarcasm in a tweet.)

 @BobMcGlory I have my complete series of investigative best-sellers: The Plot To Kill Jim Croce, The Assassination of John Denver, and Lynyrd Skynyrd: Why He Had To Die.

@CarolConnelly Is it too late to back out of this mission?

 @GeneralStone Let's all calm down. If this mission is going to succeed, we're going to have to get along. There needs to be a mutual respect.

 @BobMcGlory If Carroll is going to disrespect my books, and especially disrespect my books on tape, we will have a problem.

 @CarolConnelly Look, for the sake of the team, I will apologize for disparaging all the hard work that your ghost writer put into your books.

 @BobMcGlory Apology accepted.

 @MontyWashburn I think books are stupid.

 @BobMcGlory We're talking about books on tape, idiot!

 @MontyWashburn Wait, what? I don't get what you're saying.

 @BobMcGlory A. Book. On. Tape. It's an audio recording of the author reading his book.

 @MontyWashburn And I don't have to do any reading myself?

 @BobMcGlory No!

@MontyWashburn They have the technology to do that? Awesome!

 @BobMcGlory I want to punch you so hard right now.

 @GeneralStone Seriously? You've never heard of audio books?

 @CarolConnelly To find out he would have had to read about it.

 @MontyWashburn I don't hate all forms of reading. Just the kind that involve sentences.

 @CarolConnelly What about paragraphs?

 @MontyWashburn I especially hate long-form pieces. But here's a kind of reading I do like, and it's a fun activity for a road trip. Let's look at license plates and say how they make us feel about America.

 @BobMcGlory What?

 @MontyWashburn Look at a license plate on a passing car. Pick a state that the license plate is from. And use that state as an emblem of what you love about America.

 @CarolConnelly I love the United States Of America, and as such I also love her automobile registration bureaucracy. But this sounds like a stupid game.

 @BobMcGlory Then let's do it. If a girl thinks it's stupid, it must be worth doing.

@CarolConnelly So you're saying you can play this game without it threatening your masculinity?

 @BobMcGlory Hey, babe, I'll have you know that I have zero insecurities about my masculinity!

 @CarolConnelly Fine. Whatever.

 @BobMcGlory What do you mean by that?!!! How dare you imply that I have a small penis!

 @MontyWashburn Can we just play the game? I'm bored, so I'm in the perfect mood to express what I love about America.

 @GeneralStone Okay, just to change the conversation, there's a license plate from Tennessee. What does that make you think of?

 @BobMcGlory Ratings. My show was the highest rated in Tennessee. I am proud of that to this day.

 @GeneralStone As well you should be.

 @BobMcGlory When I went there to do a live reading of my beautiful heartwarming story, The Christmas Jockstrap, all the Tennesseans at the meet & greet afterwards were so worshipful of me.

 @BobMcGlory The fans who came to my personal appearances and paid extra for my VIP package are the true Americans.

 @CarolConnelly And the ones that didn't pay for the VIP package?

85

@BobMcGlory Secret Muslims. But now that I don't have a TV show, our country has become a post apocalyptic dystopia. All my book and personal appearance contracts have been cancelled. Those liberals! Those damn liberals! I'll make them pay! They'll pay!!!

 @GeneralStone Calm down. Keep you anger in check. You'll get your chance. Stay focused! Let's keep playing the license game. Look, there's one from Connecticut.

 @MontyWashburn Yuck! Liberal state!

 @CarolConnelly It is lovely.

 @MontyWashburn I hate it.

 @GeneralStone But we're supposed to talk about why a state makes us proud of America.

 @MontyWashburn Okay, well, what could be more patriotic than hanging a flag from the highest flag pole, right?

 @GeneralStone Right.

 @MontyWashburn Well, at the boarding school I went to, they hung me from the highest flag pole. It was the the biggest wedgie in the history of New England!

 @BobMcGlory I'm speechless.

@MontyWashburn Because you sympathize with me?

 @BobMcGlory No, because I'm laughing so hard.

 @MontyWashburn Really? Oh my God, I finally made someone laugh. It's a first in my comedy career. Thank you!

 @CarolConnelly Monty, he's not laughing with you, he's laughing at you.

 @MontyWashburn I know! It's awesome!

 @CarolConnelly Monty, I don't think you're aware that you are being bullied.

 @BobMcGlory Hey, honey, obviously you've never listened to my podcast.

 @CarolConnelly Why should I be any different from the rest of the county?

 @BobMcGlory Shut up! Just shut up! I'll have you know I did a whole rant about bullying on my podcast. I said that we have a bullying problem in this country: there's not enough of it.

 @MontyWashburn My dream is to one day be like you, Mr. McGlory - the bullied who becomes the bully.

 @BobMcGlory What are you talking about? I was never bullied! My father constantly berated me because he wanted me to be better than him, and I'm proud to say I am better than him at bullying people.

@GeneralStone Look, this game isn't fun anymore. Before we get to Aspen, let's go over a scenario I've developed for our timeline.

 @MontyWashburn Our timeline on Twitter?

 @GeneralStone No, an actual timeline that will happen in the real world.

 @MontyWashburn Is that even a thing?

 @GeneralStone Yes, but I need to tell you upfront, it's going to be in rhyme.

 @BobMcGlory Rhyme? What for?

 @GeneralStone It'll make it easier to remember. They do it in The Dirty Dozen, so I thought it might work for this mission.

 @BobMcGlory Okay, but...rhyme? Really?

 @CarolConnelly What's the problem?

 @BobMcGlory It just seems... What's the word I'm looking for?

 @MontyWashburn Gay?

@BobMcGlory I was going to say Black.

 @MontyWashburn Black?

 @BobMcGlory Yes, like rap and hip hop. But I take your point, rhyming is poetry, so it's also gay.

 @CarolConnelly What are you saying?

 @BobMcGlory I'm saying that rhyming combines black pride and gay culture, the two things I've fought against my whole life.

 @CarolConnelly You know, your racism almost distracts from your sexism. Almost.

 @BobMcGlory What are you saying?

 @CarolConnelly You hate black people!

 @BobMcGlory And hating black people makes me racist, how?

 @GeneralStone Look, please let's just all give this rhyming thing a try, okay? Here is the timeline in rhyme I came up with:

 @GeneralStone 1. We arrive in Aspen before the affair. 2. We gather our resources as we prepare.

@BobMcGlory Does this part of the rhyme scheme include checking into our hotel?

 @GeneralStone No.

 @BobMcGlory I forgot to ask what hotel we'll be staying at in Aspen.

 @GeneralStone Actually, we're not going to be staying anywhere. We're just going to get in, do the mission, and get out.

 @CarolConnelly We won't even stay at an Air BnB?

 @BobMcGlory Air BnB? That's a liberal thing! Isn't that where sleeper cells stay?

 @MontyWashburn Yes, if they're looking something more affordable than a hotel.

 @GeneralStone We will draw too much attention if we check into a hotel or an Air BnB. We need to swiftly go in and out. This is a covert operation, after all.

 @BobMcGlory It may be a covert mission, but I always expect first class hotel accommodations. It's in my Ryder.

 @GeneralStone There is no Ryder for this mission.

 @BobMcGlory What? I'm calling my agent.

@GeneralStone Involving your agency representation could undermine this entire operation. It's an undercover mission.

 @BobMcGlory And remind me once again why I'm doing an undercover mission?

 @GeneralStone It's good exposure.

 @BobMcGlory Right, I forgot.

 @GeneralStone 3. Bob and Monty enter the party, both in disguises 4. While Carol and I mingle and deal with what arises.

 @MontyWashburn This is the first party I've ever been invited to!

 @GeneralStone You weren't invited. You're going undercover, remember?

 @MontyWashburn Oh, right.

 @CarolConnelly You've never been invited to a party? That is so sad.

 @MontyWashburn I don't need your pity!

 @CarolConnelly I'm sorry.

 @MontyWashburn I don't need your pity, but I welcome it!

@CarolConnelly Well, okay, then. I feel deeply sorry for you.

 @MontyWashburn Thank you. I find pity empowering.

 @GeneralStone Continuing with the plan:

 @GeneralStone 5. The party has started and while the liberals enjoy it 6. Bob plants the bombs inside the toilet.

 @BobMcGlory I will be disguised as a janitor.

 @MontyWashburn I read an interview where you said your father was a janitor.

 @GeneralStone Don't bring up McGlory's father!

 @BobMcGlory Why not bring up my dad? Yes, he was a janitor, but he was also my hero.

 @MontyWashburn So this janitor disguise should be a natural to you.

 @BobMcGlory What are you saying? I should emulate my old man and spend all day being a janitor, then come home bitter and pissed off about it?

 @MontyWashburn No!

@BobMcGlory Then I should go to the nearest bar and drink up my entire paycheck until there's none left over for the wife and kids?

 @GeneralStone Bob, don't lose focus!

 @BobMcGlory Oh, I know, then I'll find a kid who wants to be a broadcaster, and tell him that he's no good and that he's stupid to believe he can be anything other than a janitor.

 @MontyWashburn That might require too many logistics.

 @BobMcGlory Then if this kid hands me any back sass, I'll beat him to a pulp and not give him anything on his birthday.

 @CarolConnelly I hope God forgives me for enjoying this story.

 @BobMcGlory And I'll also tell this bright young man that Santa didn't bring him anything because he's been a bad boy and Santa doesn't like him.

 @MontyWashburn Gosh, I'm sorry to hear that you had a horrible holiday experience.

 @BobMcGlory I didn't have a horrible holiday experience!!! I had a horrible Christmas experience, you Godless fuck!!!

 @GeneralStone Okay, you know what, maybe you shouldn't wear a janitor disguise if it's going to remind you of your father.

 @BobMcGlory My father? What's wrong with my father? He was a great man!

@CarolConnelly Of course.

 @BobMcGlory Shut up! Just shut up!

 @CarolConnelly I didn't say anything. I just honestly feel bad that you had an unhappy childhood.

.

 @BobMcGlory Don't knock it, baby. Unhappy childhoods are the foundation upon which all successful careers are built.

 @CarolConnelly That is actually insightful. This whole conversation is like therapy for you.

 @BobMcGlory Therapy? Stop accusing me of being gay!

 @CarolConnelly Nobody said you're gay.

 @BobMcGlory But, therapy, that's a gay thing, isn't it?

 @MontyWashburn It's gayer than some things I could name, like having anal intercourse with someone of the same sex.

 @CarolConnelly Excuse me?

 @MontyWashburn Look, even if you do gay stuff, you're never truly gay if you're a conservative.

@CarolConnelly Come again?

 @MontyWashburn No, I'll never come again, not into another man at least. Because I'm not gay. Not anymore. My therapist told me so.

 @BobMcGlory But you went to therapy, and I think we've established that therapy is gay.

 @MontyWashburn But this was gay conversion therapy.

 @BobMcGlory I'm sorry, but gay conversion therapy is gay.

 @MontyWashburn How so?

 @BobMcGlory Because it's therapy!

 @MontyWashburn Okay, fair enough. But I'm just saying that as gay as gay conversion therapy is, it did convert me and now I'm never gay. Hardly ever.

 @GeneralStone Look, the whole question of who is gay, who isn't gay, let's sort it out over drinks after the mission. In the meantime, we need to focus.

 @GeneralStone 7. While the laxatives are causing bowels to drain 8. Carol holds forth with the men who remain.

 @CarolConnelly That's right. Not everyone at the party will be sampling the mustard. So I'll express my opinion to those powerful liberal pundits and it will cause them to mansplain things to me and thus I can keep them occupied for hours if I need to.

95

@GeneralStone This is great! We'll all be working separately and yet together. Don't forget, we're a team!

 @MontyWashburn That reminds me. I've come up with a cool name for our outfit.

 @BobMcGlory Uh oh.

 @MontyWashburn No, you'll like it. Here it is...
Deployment
Of
Unified
Commando
Heterosexual
Evangelicals
Benefiting
American
Greatness

 @GeneralStone I love it!

 @BobMcGlory Hate to admit it, kid, but you've come up with a good one there.

 @CarolConnelly Does "evangelicals" accurately describe all of us?

 @GeneralStone Maybe not, but it's on brand.

 @CarolConnelly Might I just mention that one of our members is a serial sexual abuser whose moral depravity is a repudiation of every teaching in the Bible?

@BobMcGlory You don't have to point out that I continue to have the full support of Evangelical Christian leaders, we all know it already!

 @GeneralStone Let's not quibble. On to the plan. Our next step...

 @GeneralStone 9. We arrive at the party with all the swells. 10. Then detonate the bombs and unleash hell.

 @MontyWashburn We will go down in history for this.

 @BobMcGlory The network will beg for me to come back. I'll be offered millions!

 @MontyWashburn I am one laxative dose away from finally being respected as an artist.

 @CarolConnelly I'm thinking a daytime talk show is in store for me. And if my show is successful, it will open doors for one or two other women over the course of the next few decades.

 @GeneralStone And by pulling off a successful covert commando operation, I'll regain the kind of cable TV exposure that all true military men covet.

 @CarolConnelly You miss being on cable news shows, don't you?

 @GeneralStone I'd give anything to be in a green room again. I love the smell of complimentary bagels in the morning. It smells like

 @BobMcGlory Victory?

@GeneralStone I was going to say Judaism.

 @BobMcGlory There's a lot riding on this for all of us. My critics have been gloating, saying I'll never be able to sexually harass women in the workplace again. But I believe anything is possible in this great nation of ours.

PART FIVE

And now we come to the live-tweeting of the actual mission, perhaps the most damning evidence being submitted to the committee, but we'll let the Senators draw their own conclusions.

@MontyWashburn I just noticed something surprising about Aspen.

 @GeneralStone What's that?

 @MontyWashburn People seem to really be into skiing here.

 @CarolConnelly The mountains and the snow tend to encourage that sort of thing.

 @MontyWashburn Do you think I could get in a few runs in on the slopes before we start?

 @CarolConnelly Have you ever skied?

 @MontyWashburn No, but as a conservative, I feel I can always count on my innate sense of being right about everything to get me through any new endeavor.

 @GeneralStone Regardless, you can't go skiing. We are on a strict timetable.

 @MontyWashburn But when I discover something cool about a town, I enjoy partaking in it. Like, for instance, did you know that Las Vegas has legalized gambling?

 @BobMcGlory He's off the mission as of this minute, right?

 @GeneralStone It's too late for that. Let's just stick to the plan and everything will be okay. The party is starting soon.

@BobMcGlory I just got into my janitor outfit. It's so odd. Somehow, somewhere, at some point in the twentieth century, someone convinced working class men to wear jumpsuits. I don't know how it happened.

 @MontyWashburn It's exactly the kind of outfit your father used to wear, right?

 @BobMcGlory No! Don't say that! I'm not a loser!!! Don't you call me that, dad!!! I will make good, do you hear me! No, don't hit me!!! Don't hit me!!!

 @CarolConnelly Oh, my God, McGlory is having another psychotic break! Or should I say, a different kind of psychotic break than the ones he had on his TV show every day.

 @GeneralStone It must be the Janitors outfit, it's unleashing traumatic memories in him.

 @BobMcGlory No, I'm fine, I'm okay. It's a brand new suit, so I can't smell my dad's stink on it, the sweaty odor I remember from my childhood. It was the manly stench of his disapproval. It is with me always.

 @GeneralStone Are you okay?

 @BobMcGlory Yeah, I'm fine. I just walked through the kitchen entrance of the venue and I'm in.

 @GeneralStone Good, I knew those forged identification cards that I got from my connections in military intelligence would work.

 @BobMcGlory Actually, I didn't need to use them.

@GeneralStone You didn't? Why not?

 @BobMcGlory Oh, I was recognized.

 @GeneralStone You were?

 @BobMcGlory Yeah, and I signed autographs.

 @GeneralStone But you're supposed to be covert. No one can know who you really are!

 @BobMcGlory Then I guess you're not going to like that I set up a merch table in the pantry.

 @GeneralStone Why in God's name would you do that?!!!

 @BobMcGlory To sell books and mugs and T shirts. That's standard practice on a commando mission, right?

 @GeneralStone No it isn't!!!

 @BobMcGlory Relax, this town is lousy with liberals, so I didn't sell much, but I did meet a fan. She works as a dishwasher in the kitchen of this place.

 @GeneralStone This is not a good development. And I'm surprised you met a fan of yours in Aspen.

@BobMcGlory Well, to be honest, she's not exactly a fan. She's an illegal, and I told her if she didn't help me I'd turn her ass in. And I made her preorder my next book, The Man Who Shot Freddy Prinze.

 @CarolConnelly He shot himself.

 @BobMcGlory Exactly! Leave it to a no good hispanic to kill a beloved star like Freddy Prinze!

 @GeneralStone Bob, you're being too conspicuous! Stay undercover!

 @BobMcGlory Hey, don't worry, nobody recognizes me where I am right now. I'm just a janitor as far as they are concerned.

 @GeneralStone Good.

 @BobMcGlory But if they do recognize me, I'll see if I can get them to subscribe to my podcast.

 @GeneralStone Look, if we succeed here, you won't need to do a podcast anymore. That's the whole point of this operation.

 @BobMcGlory If this mission means I no longer have to do a podcast, that makes it the most consequential commando mission in the history of America!

 @CarolConnelly Hey, you guys should see the evening gown I'm wearing. It's pretty nice.

 @BobMcGlory This is no time for hyperbole, honey.

@MontyWashburn Sorry, gang, but no evening gown or janitor outfit can compare to my costume. It is awesome!

 @GeneralStone Don't forget, you're supposed to be in disguise.

 @MontyWashburn I am in disguise! We know from the intelligence you've gathered that George Clooney is going to be at the party, and the party-goers are going to think I'm George Clooney!

 @GeneralStone How exactly are you pulling that off?

 @MontyWashburn I'm wearing a Batman costume!

 @GeneralStone What?!!!

 @MontyWashburn Don't worry, nobody is going to think I'm Val Kilmer. They're all gonna be convinced that I'm George Clooney.

 @GeneralStone I think they're going to think George Clooney is George Clooney.

 @MontyWashburn But I'm telling you, my Batman costume looks just like George Clooney. So when they see the real George Clooney, wearing a tuxedo and looking all like George Clooney, they'll think he's an imposter.

 @GeneralStone I honestly don't think this a good idea.

@MontyWashburn Well, I'm sorry, I'm not getting out of this Batman costume. It is essential to my plan, plus, the rubber lycra feels sensual against my balls.

 @CarolConnelly What about the nipples?

 @MontyWashburn That's the part of the costume that really sells the idea that I'm George Clooney in Batman & Robin.

 @GeneralStone Okay, you can wear the costume, as long as we can stop having this discussion.

 @BobMcGlory Hey, if you don't mind talking to me about the mission, I just thought I'd inform you that I'm in the bathroom and I'm planting the bombs.

 @GeneralStone In the chateau?

 @BobMcGlory I'm not going to call it some poopie frenchy thing like "chateau." I don't use French terms. When I was cheating on my wife, I never had a rendezvous, I had a hook up, because that's the American Way!

 @CarolConnelly I can see the "out of order" sign you put in front of the bathroom door. This place is starting to fill up with progressive elites.

 @CarolConnelly I see politicians, pundits, celebrities, all dressed in the kind of expensive designer clothing you'd expect from such passionate advocates for the poor and downtrodden.

 @MontyWashburn Gosh, you have genuine contempt for them don't you?

@CarolConnelly Yes, and it's causing them to flock to me. Disdain is a perfume that attracts liberal guilt.

 @GeneralStone Then you're doing what you claimed you could do on this mission. Kudos for that.

 @CarolConnelly Well, I just want to be treated like an equal on this commando team and not be condescended to.

 @GeneralStone That's so precious. Good girl!

 @CarolConnelly Whatever. This whole cavernous space has the feel of a warm, woodsy, humble, down-to-earth ski lodge with a million dollar membership fee.

 @BobMcGlory And yet there are people of color everywhere. The Democrats have no concept of exclusivity, which is why they can never be the party of all the people.

 @CarolConnelly Well, it looks like I'm about to strike up a conversation with Maurice Antoinette, the designer of the new Grey Poupon.

 @MontyWashburn I imagine a guy like that is pretty stuck up, huh?

 @CarolConnelly Well, he is a bit haughty.

 @CarolConnelly He's bald except for a single spit curl in the middle of his forehead. He's dressed in a ruffled outfit that looks like it would have been too ostentatious for the Sgt. Pepper's album cover, and his upper eyelids are droopy, probably from looking down his nose so often.

@BobMcGlory Jeez, you're really into this guy, aren't you? Why don't you just marry him?

 @CarolConnelly Sure, it would give you something new to judge.

 @BobMcGlory Hey, babe, I'm not judging anyone. I just don't think weirdoes should get married.

 @CarolConnelly Yes, your experience has led you to believe that marriage is something that's strictly between a man and his lawyer, right?

 @BobMcGlory Just shut up and do your job. I'm still worried that having a girl along will ruin this mission.

 @CarolConnelly You know, in addition to the sign outside the bathroom, someone should hang an "out of order" sign on your psyche.

 @GeneralStone Stay focused, everyone. Stay focused.

 @CarolConnelly I am focused! I've struck up a conversation with Maurice Antoinette. He is quite susceptible to flattery. I just called him the auteur of mustard and when he's not asking an assistant to transcribe his every thought, he's hanging on my every word.

 @BobMcGlory I did a report on him years ago. He tried to open a Ministry of French Condiments during the Obama Administration.

 @CarolConnelly That was a story you reported with no sources and no confirmation that it was remotely true.

@BobMcGlory Yup, it met all the journalistic standards of my network and it was a great report!

 @GeneralStone Stay close to Maurice Antoinette, Carol. You need to keep him occupied so Monty can slip the laxative into the bowls of Grey Poupon mustard.

 @CarolConnelly Okay, but one problem I'm having is that there are a lot of media figures here trying to make eye contact with me.

 @GeneralStone You already know a lot of them, don't you?

 @CarolConnelly Yes, many have invited me to come to their houses to watch them take showers.

 @BobMcGlory That is so wrong!

 @CarolConnelly YOU'RE ranting against sexual harassment?

 @BobMcGlory I'm just pointing out that I was the first TV pundit to introduce the idea of bathroom cleaning supplies into employer/employee sex and I never get any credit.

 @GeneralStone Let's not get bogged down in intellectual property disputes. Monty, have you spiked the mustard?

 @MontyWashburn I'm not in the building yet. I'm outside posing for pictures with Batman fans.

 @GeneralStone For God's sake, get in the building! Time is running out and you've got to get the ex-lax into the Grey Poupon!

@CarolConnelly Maurice Antonette just offered me an appetizer with the new mustard upgrade on it.

 @MontyWashburn You poor thing.

 @CarolConnelly It's actually pretty good.

 @BobMcGlory Traitor! She's turning on us!

 @CarolConnelly I'm just saying I am delightfully surprised at how good the mustard tasted on Swedish meatballs.

 @BobMcGlory Oh, my God! She has Stockholm Syndrome!

 @CarolConnelly Don't you mean Streisand Syndrome? Because Babs just arrived and I am only a few feet from her.

 @MontyWashburn Streisand? Are you kidding me?!!! Oh my God, Oh my God, Oh my God!!!

 @BobMcGlory What are you so excited about?

 @MontyWashburn Nothing! I despise her. She sucks.

 @BobMcGlory She represents everything we hate.

@MontyWashburn She certainly does. Do you think she'll do any songs from Yentl? Or will she open with a Marvin Hamlisch/Alan & Marilyn Bergman medley?

 @BobMcGlory What do you care?

 @MontyWashburn I don't! And whether she's singing songs from Sondheim's Sunday In The Park With George, or dipping into the Harold Arlen catalogue, it's not anything I have any interest in.

 @CarolConnelly Gosh, Monty, I pegged you as kind of dumb, but you're actually smarter than I thought.

 @MontyWashburn I told you I'M NOT GAY!

 @CarolConnelly Regardless, let's hope Streisand does perform. Everybody at the party will be focused on her, giving us freer reign to implement our plan.

 @GeneralStone Regardless of whether she sings or not, there may be a problem with the Moderate Democrat Equivocators League.

 @CarolConnelly What's the matter?

 @GeneralStone They won't stand still. They're moving all over the place, trying to find common ground with the other party goers. They're irritating the hell out of everyone.

 @CarolConnelly Is this situation an immediate danger to our mission?

@GeneralStone It could be. Orville Pantalomur just led the group in a discussion about whether he should have a cocktail weenie or a finger sandwich. He said he wanted to hear all points of view before he made a decision.

 @CarolConnelly It looks like some guests might actually leave the party to avoid having to talk to him.

 @GeneralStone Yes, there are many prominent Democrats at this party, and they're afraid that if they go on the record about hors d'oeuvres it will come back to haunt them in the primaries.

 @CarolConnelly Hope you can get it under control. I've got my hands full with Maurice Antonette. He's afraid that Streisand is overshadowing the mustard. I tried to tell him that no singer, no matter how great, can upstage a condiment. He did not seem reassured.

 @GeneralStone Oh, crap, now the equivocators are trying to reach a consensus about whether they should mingle near the bar or by the buffet table. Another problem is that if history is any indication, whatever happens with these guys will happen incrementally.

 @MontyWashburn I just entered the building.

 @GeneralStone I know. Your Batman costume sticks out like a sore cod piece. Not exactly undercover, is it? Everyone is looking at you.

 @MontyWashburn Everyone always looks at George Clooney when he enters a room.

 @GeneralStone Nobody thinks you're George Clooney! They're more likely to think you're Rosemary Clooney.

@CarolConnelly And speaking of crooners, Streisand is about to sing.

 @MontyWashburn Oh my God, I'm here just in time. If fabulousness can kill, I'm going to die right now!

 @BobMcGlory What?!!!

 @MontyWashburn I mean, she sucks, who cares, whatever.

 @BobMcGlory Seems to me you are quite the Streisand fanboy, Monty.

 @MontyWashburn No! I mean, I used to like her, but I had I had the Babs prayed away. Now I'm just occasionally Strei-curious.

 @GeneralStone Be confused on your own time! Your job is to spike the mustard with laxative, Batman!

 @MontyWashburn I'm not Batman, I'm George Clooney!

 @CarolConnelly Well, guess what, dreamboat, Streisand just announced that she's going to sing Papa Can You Hear Me?

 @MontyWashburn From Yentl!!!! Oh my God, Oh my God, Oh my God! I mean, who gives a shit? Who gives a shit? Who gives a shit? I'm hyperventilating.

 @BobMcGlory Hey, I'm still installing the bombs, I hope I don't have to be distracted by any singing. I object to show tunes on moral grounds.

@CarolConnelly She just started singing. Man, she still has great pipes!

 @BobMcGlory Give me a break. She sounds like liberalism with a wide octave range. Her singing voice is going to come and take our guns.

 @MontyWashburn This Batman mask, it's so sweaty. For the record, that's why it looks like tears are streaming down my face.

 @BobMcGlory What do these lyrics even mean? "Papa can you hear me?" I mean, what the fuck?

 @GeneralStone Stay focused.

 @BobMcGlory Why does she keep repeating "Papa can you hear me?"

 @GeneralStone Don't lose your cool.

 @BobMcGlory I'm not losing my cool. But still, I want to know, PAPA CAN YOU HEAR ME?

 @GeneralStone You are in the middle of a mission, this is no time to be writing things in ALL CAPS.

 @GeneralStone Shit, I just did it myself.

 @CarolConnelly He's not just tweeting that. I can hear McGlory yelling "papa can you hear me?" from the bathroom.

@GeneralStone Me too. It's directing attention your way and we don't want that right now.

 @BobMcGlory Papa, I need you to hear me! Forgive me, father! I never measured up, did I?

 @GeneralStone We never should have let him get in that Janitors uniform.

 @BobMcGlory Just send me a sign, papa! Please give me your approval!

 @CarolConnelly McGlory, I guess it's okay if you tweet this, but stop yelling it! Everyone can hear you!

 @BobMcGlory Who cares if people can hear me?!!! You're not my papa! PAPA CAN YOU HEAR ME?!!!

 @MontyWashburn Everyone can hear you. You're even distracting Streisand. That's sacrilege. I mean, if you care about that kind of thing. Which I don't.

 @CarolConnelly McGlory, I can hear you crying while you punch words into your phone.

 @BobMcGlory I'm not crying! You're just like my papa! Why do you disapprove of me?

 @CarolConnelly Well, let's start with the sexual harassment...

 @BobMcGlory I realize now that I only masturbated in front of you to win approval from my father.

@CarolConnelly Wow, you're having a real emotional breakthrough, and it's making me sick to my stomach.

 @BobMcGlory Are you saying I'm being vulnerable?

 @CarolConnelly I guess in your own disgusting way, yes, you are being vulnerable.

 @BobMcGlory Well, shut up, because I am never vulnerable. Not even in the ratings! Everyone said my show was vulnerable to Rachel Maddow, but we kicked her ass in viewers aged 65 to dead!

 @GeneralStone Bob, you're getting distracted!

 @BobMcGlory We never lost the hospice demographic!

 @GeneralStone Just finish planting the bombs! Quickly!

 @BobMcGlory They're planted and ready to go.

 @MontyWashburn Good, because during this kerfuffle, I took the opportunity to slip the laxative into the big bowl of Grey Poupon. Everyone is spreading it onto their food.

 @GeneralStone There's a look of reverence on everyone's face. Sampling a new designer mustard is the closest they'll ever come to reliving the promise of the Obama Administration.

 @CarolConnelly When will the laxative kick in?

@MontyWashburn Immediately. It's a new kind that's fast acting product. Poop-inducing technology has advanced so much in recent years.

 @CarolConnelly You're right! It's already working. Everyone is rushing to the bathroom.

 @BobMcGlory Good! They'll be right in the path of the bombs when they go off.

 @GeneralStone But their path is suddenly being blocked by someone.

 @CarolConnelly The person blocking their path isn't just someone. IT'S OPRAH!

 @GeneralStone That flowing white gown she's wearing looks bigger than the Rockefeller Center Christmas Tree.

 @CarolConnelly And Steadman just emerged from underneath it. I guess she had to sneak him in.

 @BobMcGlory Typical liberals! They'll cry about the poor and then nickel and dime you when you request a plus-one!

 @GeneralStone Why is Oprah blocking everyone's path to the bathroom?

 @CarolConnelly She's saying, "I know you feel you are all about to shit yourselves. Well, I'm about to shit myself, too!"

 @MontyWashburn Wow, I bet Steadman is glad he got the hell out of there.

 @GeneralStone Oprah is screwing up our plan! We want those guests as close to the bombs as possible!

117

@CarolConnelly Now she's saying, "If we need to shit ourselves, it means the universe wants us to shit ourselves and we should not question the trajectory of the universe."

 @MontyWashburn That's right out of "The Secret."

 @BobMcGlory If anything should be The Secret and stay The Secret, it's when you get diarrhea.

 @CarolConnelly Oprah has inspired everyone to hug each other. She is saying, "Fill your hearts with love while you fill your pants with shit!"

 @GeneralStone So now dozens of guests with diarrhea are NOT going to make a mad dash to the bathroom like we hoped.

 @CarolConnelly And George Clooney has just entered the party.

 @MontyWashburn Ha, ha, I fooled you, didn't I? It's not George Clooney, it's me.

 @CarolConnelly No, I'm quite sure I'm looking straight at George Clooney. He's wearing a tuxedo and he's debonair and handsome as fuck.

 @MontyWashburn Is that any way for a Christian to talk?

 @CarolConnelly A Christian looking straight at George Clooney? Hell, yes! Even the Virgin Mary would say, "Yeah, I'd tap that."

 @MontyWashburn But I keep telling you, I'm not George Clooney, I'm disguised as George Clooney as Batman.

@CarolConnelly Well, some guy who looks exactly like George Clooney as George Clooney is behind you and staring right at you!

 @MontyWashburn You're right! George Clooney thinks I'm George Clooney. That's how good my George Clooney cosplay is!

 @CarolConnelly He is staring intensely at you. It looks like he's about to scream!

 @BobMcGlory He is screaming. I can hear it down here. I skedaddled out of the bathroom and now I'm in the basement. What's he saying?

 @CarolConnelly He's looking straight at Monty and saying: "Go away! Why must you haunt me! Be gone with you, Ghost!"

 @MontyWashburn I am totally freaking him out.

 @CarolConnelly He's saying, "Why must you always torment me, Ghost of Schumacher! Haven't I atoned for my original sin? I've done good works. I've made good movies. Yet I star in Batman & Robin and it haunts me forever! Please release me from your curse!"

 @GeneralStone And now Streisand has stopped singing and is moving towards Clooney.

 @CarolConnelly She just said, "George, what's the matter? We all love you. What can you possibly think you've done that's so unforgivable?"

 @GeneralStone He replied, "I starred in Batman & Robin."

@CarolConnelly Babs just said, "Oh, right. Yeah, that is an awful thing to have done. Even my followers thought it was too campy, and they're fucking Barbara Streisand fans."

 @GeneralStone Clooney is grabbing his hair and saying, "This ghost won't stop tormenting me and following me around."

 @MontyWashburn Now he's screaming and running out of the building.

 @BobMcGlory Crap, he'll miss the blast. We won't get to kill him.

 @GeneralStone Kill him? What are you talking about?

 @BobMcGlory I planted the bombs. The building is about to blow up.

 @GeneralStone No it isn't.

 @BobMcGlory Yes it is, I just told you the explosives have been planted.

 @GeneralStone But they're not going to blow up the building. That would kill everybody.

 @BobMcGlory That's the whole idea, isn't it?

 @GeneralStone No, they're not real bombs. They're stink bombs. They're supposed to be stink bombs.

@BobMcGlory This is the first I'm hearing of it.

 @GeneralStone The idea was to embarrass them. To own the libs by making them act in a way that would cause them to be ridiculed on Twitter for a day and thus induce permanent damage. We never had any intention of killing these people.

 @BobMcGlory But they're liberals.

 @GeneralStone That's not enough of a reason to kill them!

 @BobMcGlory I have lost all respect for you.

 @GeneralStone We have to stop the mission now! Abort! Abort!

 @BobMcGlory You know how I feel about abortion. I'm against it. Except in the case of interns I knocked up.

 @GeneralStone I meant abort the mission. Defuse the bombs!

 @BobMcGlory Can't do it, they're set to go kablooey and there's nothing to be done except for us to hightail it out of here.

 @GeneralStone We need to evacuate everyone from the building!

 @BobMcGlory Are you sure? Can't we let at least some of the liberals die?

@GeneralStone No! We must evacuate!

@CarolConnelly Everyone is already evacuating their bowels.

@MontyWashburn Streisand just ran over to me and said, "Leave Clooney alone, Caped Crusader!" Jeez, who does she think I am, Adam West? I am so disillusioned. Let's leave her to die.

@GeneralStone No, we have to get everyone out before the bombs go off.

@BobMcGlory So now you're trying to save lives? What kind of a military man are you?

@GeneralStone I don't care what their political affiliations are. The law clearly states that you can't kill celebrities.

@BobMcGlory Well, I thought indiscriminately killing people we disagree with was the whole point of this mission. But I guess I'm just an idealist.

@CarolConnelly And I thought it was just the criminal sexual abuse that made you morally reprehensible. Huh, live and learn.

@GeneralStone No one is going to live unless we get everyone out of here.

@GeneralStone I just told the Moderate Democratic Centrist Equivocators that they're in mortal danger. I thought they were all going to be paralyzed with indecision but then they looked at the street outside and instinctively ran towards the middle of the road.

@CarolConnelly There is suddenly a huge commotion caused by a ferocious noise that's making everyone run for the door. What is that?

 @BobMcGlory That's me. I'm yelling "WE'LL DO IT NUDE! WE'LL DO IT NUDE!"

 @GeneralStone That's from the infamous viral video where you screamed on camera about how feminine your suit looked in the monitor.

 @BobMcGlory Well, it did! I'll tell you one thing, they had no right calling themselves a MENS warehouse.

 @GeneralStone Well, go ahead and keep screaming "we'll do it nude" over and over again because you're saving lives. It's terrifying, but it's working. Everyone is running out of the building.

 @CarolConnelly Did everyone on our team make it outside?

 @MontyWashburn I did.

 @GeneralStone I'm out.

 @BobMcGlory Everyone is out of the building and this whole mission is now officially a bust.

 @MontyWashburn The building is exploding. You really did a good job with the explosives, Mr. McGlory.

 @BobMcGlory I tried to make a difference.

@MontyWashburn We did make a difference. Look! A bunch of liberals are squatting in the street, spraying diarrhea all over the ground while sobbing because they were almost just killed.

 @GeneralStone Snowflakes.

 @BobMcGlory I know, right? Bunch of wimps.

 @GeneralStone No, I meant a bunch of snowflakes are falling to the ground.

 @CarolConnelly The smoke from the explosion is turning the snowflakes brown.

 @GeneralStone Like Grey Poupon mustard!

 @CarolConnelly Yes, in fact, the air smells like Grey Poupon.

 @BobMcGlory It's literally snowing Grey Poupon mustard on Aspen right now. We've created a liberal paradise.

 @MontyWashburn God, we suck.

PART SIX

The mission completed, the subjects of our investigation continued to interact with each other on Twitter.

@BobMcGlory Well, thanks a lot, General. You recruited me for this so-called commando raid, and now I'm throughly fucked.

 @GeneralStone What are you talking about? Time Magazine just named us Persons if the Year.

 @BobMcGlory Yeah, I saw that article, and I'm ruined!

 @GeneralStone Did you see the copy?
"For doing more to bridge the bipartisan gap by saving the lives of those on the opposite side of the political spectrum, we name the D. O. U. C. H. E. B. A. G. team our persons of the year."

 @BobMcGlory That's another thing, Now that I've seen it in print, I don't like our commando team name anymore.

 @GeneralStone But this whole caper put us all back into the zeitgeist.

 @BobMcGlory Hey, don't use those fancy French words with me. I was living the simple life of a podcaster known to the world as a disgraced sexual abuser. And now that's all been ruined.

 @GeneralStone How so?

 @BobMcGlory Liberals love me now. I'm their hero because they think I showed compassion and love for the other side. I saved George Clooney's life. I saved Barbara Streisand's life. I saved Oprah's life. I can't even say this out loud, it makes me so ashamed.

 @GeneralStone But you're no longer ostracized by the media. Isn't that what you wanted?

@BobMcGlory Not this way! I'm welcome to go on The View anytime I want. Rachel Maddow did an eighteen minute segment on how much she admires me. She didn't get to her point until the last few seconds, but her point was clear. Eventually.

 @GeneralStone Are you really saying that no good came from this?

 @BobMcGlory Well, the Green Party wants me to run for President, but that's the only Republican support I've gotten. Overall, conservative media will have nothing to do with me. They say I'm a sellout.

 @GeneralStone I'm sorry to hear this.

 @BobMcGlory What do you care? You're back on top in the cable news world.

 @GeneralStone Yes, it's true. My new reputation as a man of peace has inspired CNN to hire me back as an advocate for war.

 @MontyWashburn Lucky for you. At least you weren't sued by Warner Brothers and DC Comics.

 @GeneralStone For the Batman cosplay?

 @MontyWashburn Some people found my appearance as Batman entertaining, so the movie division of Warner Brothers is saying I've harmed their brand.

 @CarolConnelly So you have to avoid being entertaining?

 @MontyWashburn Yes, that's why I've started doing stand up comedy again.

@CarolConnelly Good luck with that. I've got some good news. All this publicity is getting me back into the TV news business.

 @GeneralStone Congratulations!

 @CarolConnelly Vice Media wants to go after the young Christianity market so they've hired me to be the main anchor on their new startup network called Vice/Christ.

 @GeneralStone Congratulations, but I have to ask, does a channel that combines vice and Christianity make any sense?

 @CarolConnelly Makes about as much sense as anything else going on in this crazy world right now.

 @GeneralStone Fair point.

 @CarolConnelly Whatever the challenges, I hope to communicate and make a positive difference in the lives of young people.

 @BobMcGlory Well, bully for you.

 @CarolConnelly Bob, you seem a little bitter and jealous.

 @BobMcGlory That's a lie, you opportunistic bitch cunt twat whore.

 @CarolConnelly Hey back off, you're being a jerk.

Twitter note: Abusive, vulgar hate speech is a violation of our Terms of Service, which is why we have banned Carol Connelly from Twitter.

Upon reviewing the evidence presented, especially the Twitter feed, the Senate Committee has reached some conclusions.

General Stone was the instigator of this mission and as such is the one who should be held most responsible for putting innocent civilians at risk. But we've met with him on several occasions and have concluded that he is a really nice guy. This therefore mitigates any danger he may have caused and we recommend that anyone on this committee having a cocktail party should invite him along because he does indeed have considerable social skills, which as you know is quite important here in Washington, D.C.

As for Carol Connelly, she is a journalist, and one with a noticeable conservative bent. However there is a matter that she seems to have done little to rectify: she's a woman. Also, she seems to have a basic distrust of men despite the considerable effort we've put into pretending to treat her as an equal.

There is also the matter of the considerable trauma she caused to our friend and colleague, Mike Pence. This is a bit out of our jurisdiction, but we are advocating that the Surgeon General and the World Heath Organization increase their efforts to deal with the scourge of Girl Cooties.

Monty Washburn, to our surprise, has emerged as a unifying figure in this investigation. For the first time in our nation's history, the entirety of the United States Congress has joined forces to declare by proclamation that Monty Washburn is officially not funny. This has already resulted in him being asked to write a Shouts and Murmurs piece for the New Yorker.

Bob McGlory has always been controversial, and this incident has made him a heroic figure to the general public, but our investigation reveals a different story: he willfully planted explosives at a public venue with the clear intention of taking the lives of innocent Americans.

But like we said, he is a heroic figure to the general public, and as such his situation must be carefully finessed. So while his behavior must be condemned in no uncertain terms, we recommend that the members of this committee do so in the privacy of your homes to whichever of your most cherished loved ones are willing to sign a non disclosure agreement.

In this world of social media and mass communications, we need to maintain our reputation as a party that isn't afraid to speak out on matters of morality and family values, so the best course of action is to keep our fucking mouths shut.

Thus concludes our investigation into this matter.

Made in the USA
Middletown, DE
15 August 2018